SCUBA DIVING

SCUBA DIVING

Joan Deakin

David & Charles
Newton Abbot   London

British Library Cataloguing in Publication Data

Deakin, Joan
  Scuba diving.
  1. Scuba diving
  I. Title
  797.2'3   GV840.S78

  ISBN 0–7153–7952–6

Set by Northern Phototypesetting Company Bolton
and printed in Great Britain by
Redwood Burn Limited Trowbridge and Esher
for David & Charles (Publishers) Limited
Brunel House Newton Abbot Devon

Contents

List of Illustrations

1
A General Introduction

There is something strange and wonderful about dropping slowly feet first through clear water, your bubbles rising above you towards the sunlit surface. You are truly making a journey into another world. One which is completely peaceful where none of the strident everyday sounds can reach you. There is the absolute minimum of signalled communication between you and your buddy. The sensation of rolling backwards off the gunwales of a boat at the start of a visit to an unknown destination is unique and never palls. No matter where you dive or in what depth of water there will always be life of some kind. You may be seeing it for the hundredth time but somehow that does not detract from the experience. Cool, exhilarated, you fin lazily along trying to become part of the environment. Looking, pausing, touching, impressing each detail upon your mind. There is never enough time. You start to go up, finning strongly to leave the seabed. As you rise you feel the pressure of the water on your body decrease and you keep your rate of ascent to that of the small bubbles which rise above you so that you do not go up into the 'real' world too quickly for safety.

Man has been diving underwater since hundreds of years BC without mechanical aids but it was during the sixteenth century that an Italian designed and built the first diving bell which was actually usable underwater. From then on man's desire to visit, and even work, under the sea meant that the invention and trial of suitable practical aids to this end went on in various parts of the world. It continued with different types of bells until, in 1816, an open diving dress was produced by a German named Siebe. This 'open' dress permitted the diver to be supplied with air direct from the surface via an airline and was the first opportunity man had for walking about on the seabed. In 1837 Siebe improved on his design.

Time passed with more inventions and changes in diving equipment until eventually, in 1860, two Frenchmen designed the first diving regulator. Unfortunately for them, although the regulator was good in principle and was the forerunner of the ones used today, there were not, at that time, cylinders available which were light enough having a large enough capacity. This meant that the cylinders used, 30atm pressure rating, had to be topped up from the surface via an airline and thus the diver was still tied to a certain radius. Development did not proceed at that time.

In the 1940s cylinders light enough and large enough were available and another Frenchman designed a free diving set. The drawback was that the air had to be regulated manually. Jacques Cousteau had already carried out experiments in the 1930s and now tried this set. He decided that the diver needed to be fed on demand. This led to a working partnership between himself and a man named Emile Gagnan. Between them they produced a demand valve and opened the doors to a new sport and a new world by giving us the 'aqualung' or self-contained underwater breathing apparatus (scuba).

Not only did he and his partner give us the means to visit it, but Jacques Cousteau and his diving team brought the world into our homes in glorious colour, through the medium of fascinating films on television and books packed with photographs of the enchanting life beneath the sea in various parts of the globe. Other people too have fired the imagination with their searches for lost ships filled with treasure, painstaking recovery of ancient underwater sites and experiments with modern reconstructions of equipment long since consigned to the history books.

Since the beginning of time the sea has lured man to set sail in puny vessels for other lands. She claims her victims yearly, without mercy. Even now, with the aid of every modern device, ships go down to lie on reefs or to lie scattered across the seabed. They lie in a few metres or in many. In areas where the tides are so fierce there is only a little time each day when a dive may be carried out. They may be flung against reefs where the surge of the water can have a dangerous and unnerving effect on a diver. The small ancient ships have long since been reduced to matchwood, the later iron ships gradually have become twisted heaps of scrap metal, just recognisable as something once proud and grand which lost its battle with the ocean.

Many of these wrecks have been found after months and sometimes years of research in libraries, museums and charts. After that comes the search at sea, sometimes years of investigating the likely area – akin to looking for a needle in a haystack. The likelihood is that the action of the sea has taken the wreck, or part of it, outside the area in which the ship was thought to have gone down. Ancient wrecks are particularly difficult to find. Centuries of sand or mud cover the wooden structure and, luckily, in some cases can help to preserve some of the timbers in quite good condition. The wreck will usually have disappeared completely and has to be recovered by excavation.

Having discovered the site, which may be found merely as a 'sub-mud feature', the excavation begins. Trenches are dug and lines laid out so that every centimetre of the seabed can be systematically sifted for artifacts, pieces of timber, etc, until the exact position and lie of the ship can be ascertained. The artifacts help to prove the identity of the ship by confirming its age, origin, etc. Depending on the depth you can spend quite long periods almost on one spot carefully digging in the mud with gloved hands or fanning away fine sand from a potentially delicate artifact. The most minute piece of pottery or wood can have some meaning to the archaeologist and has to be retrieved. Once ashore all the items have to be treated carefully to remove the corrosive salts and this again takes place over a long period.

Only then is it safe to expose the items to the fresh air of the auction rooms or museums.

Numerous 'treasure' ships have been traced and their cargoes recovered together with cannon and artifacts of a fascinating and sometimes valuable nature. Countless numbers of rare English coins, Spanish American and coins of the Netherlands, in good condition with dates clearly decipherable even after centuries at the bottom of the ocean, have been retrieved. Also whole shiploads of rare and ancient pottery, sadly reduced to sherds which have to be sorted and matched into individual pieces of pottery; barrel loads of Manillas (slave tokens) each one exchangeable for one human being; buttons of bone, copper, brass, gold and silver; silver and brass buckles; dinner ware, wine jars and bottles, some miraculously in one piece; lead shot, navigation instruments, clay pipes and hundreds of other different items, some rare and elegant pieces of work. Fortunes have been brought to the surface but only after long periods of sheer hard work and disappointments; of running risks diving regularly, day after day weather permitting, often in deep water or strong tides.

You may always want to dive just for the joy of being underwater. Sweating in a wetsuit, loading seemingly endless pieces of equipment on to a boat. Out at sea, spray sparkling in the sun. Waiting impatiently while others dive first. Watching the distorted figures move away and down through the water and their bubbles of exhausted compressed air rising like parachutes from the deep. Starting off very small all those metres below, they expand continuously until, near the surface, some of them appear to be ten centimetres or more across. All have tiny bubbles clinging around the edge like a frill. At the surface they break with a slooshing sound as they become one with the mass of water surrounding them. Kitting-up, confusion as you try to find your gear which is, mysteriously, all over the boat instead of in the original neat pile. At last, hampered by your fins you can waddle to the side of the boat. Position yourself with care, hold your mask and mouthpiece in place, and roll backwards over the gunwales. One hand on the line, finning strongly head first down through the water, to spend as much of the time allowed as possible actually on the iron wreck. As you go the pressure increases on your body, compressing your wetsuit, you feel heavier. You equalise the pressure on your ears. Watching your depth gauge you adjust your buoyancy to reduce the rate of your descent near the bottom. Weird shapes may loom up to meet you. Clouds of fish surround you, changing direction continuously. Swim up the vast dark shape of the hull, along eerie rows of portholes, some with lights still intact. Peer into the black shadows of the hold. Stare up at the massive prop. Thick plant life may have so far claimed it that the wreck has become part of the environment, barely recognisable as a ship.

The study of marine life is a leisurely and absorbing way of spending your time underwater. It is up to you whether you admire and pass by or if you want to make a closer inspection. Notes on an underwater slate may help you to make identifications later in reference books of which there is a good selection on the market. Your memory does not always retain colours and/or sizes, arrangement of stripes, etc. Obscure notes on a slate may not be sufficient to ensure positive identification. Underwater photography is a superb way of building up a record of sea life. It is, in effect, a double hobby as to obtain first-class photographs of fish or plant life a great deal of patient study of the subjects is required. To obtain true colours you may have to use flash or strobe lights unless the visibility is exceptional. If you want to invest your time and money in it you can bring back results which really are worth putting on display. Cine filming requires a different approach altogether but is especially rewarding of the time and concentration demanded. It is no good using the camera to take 'snaps', you have to go underwater with a theme in mind and film accordingly. Once filmed and developed many interesting hours can be spent on dark wet evenings editing to give the finished product a real sense of continuity and atmosphere.

11

Once you are an experienced diver all sorts of little underwater jobs can crop up in which you become involved. Putting down moorings for boatowners, finding lost objects, etc. The latter can be a complete waste of time unless the owner has marked the spot with a buoy or at least taken proper bearings. Too often the lost anchor has gone down and the owner waves a vague arm which takes in a vast area of sea and says 'it went down somewhere around here'. However, it is all experience.

Before using aqualung equipment it is essential to undergo a course of training. Generally speaking anyone who is reasonably fit will be safe to dive but it is wise, and sometimes required by clubs and schools, to have a medical. This will confirm that you have no problems with ears, sinuses, lungs, heart and blood pressure. If you are vastly overweight you will have to consider losing some of it as you will be putting strain on your heart and lungs which have to be fit for the exertions required in diving. If you are suffering from an illness which necessitates regular use of drugs this may preclude you from diving. Naturally any disability possibly causing unconsciousness underwater, such as epilepsy, also stops you from diving. Bad claustrophobia will be a hazard to a diver for obvious reasons. Mild cases will not find it a handicap – it may just mean you are not keen on very deep water or perhaps low visibility wreck diving.

The conditions causing temporary unfitness for diving should be mentioned. If you have been working exceptionally hard and are exhausted you must consider cancelling your dive. If you do dive then it should be in comparatively shallow water say, under twenty metres. The conditions underwater should not require you to exert yourself beyond normal finning (eg no strong tides). You should surface within the time and not attempt a decompression dive. If you have a hangover it is sensible to avoid diving. A very bad bout of seasickness will leave you too weak to be safe underwater, although mild nausea is experienced by many divers and should disappear as soon as you are in the water. A cold or other respiratory trouble will prevent you from diving temporarily due to the possibility of damaging the eardrums, sinuses or eustachian tubes.

Having confirmed your physical fitness you should consider your mental attitude. Your reason for learning to dive is important. Is it purely because you want to be able to say you are a diver? You like the idea of striding around in a wetsuit with a knife strapped to your leg. Is it because all your friends have started learning? Most people are sensible in their approach to diving. They have had their appetite whetted by films, books and TV documentaries. They want to visit this underwater world for themselves and are prepared to take the necessary training to ensure they can do so safely. Training also has the advantage of bringing you into contact with other novices and experienced divers, particularly if you join a club. This way you can generally find someone with whom to dive, who shares your particular interest.

When training, listen to and watch the instructor. Concentrate. Remember whatever he tells you, it will be essential knowledge on which to build up experience, gradually. Diving is a practical sport. In other words, providing you are reasonably fit, can swim, and have plenty of commonsense you have a good chance of becoming a safe diver, after thorough training. There is a fair amount of theory which must be learnt but this is taken stage by stage. As you go you can relate it to the practical aspects of the training.

The theory includes physics and physiology in relation to diving. It makes clear how your body and the compressed air you breathe reacts to pressure and what hazards are involved. Theory also explains the function of the equipment and its care. You can revise the theory taught to you but do not be afraid to ask for clarification of any points you do not understand fully. It is vital that you do not finish your training before you have a full grasp of all the facts. The practical side starts you off with mask, fins and snorkel and leads on to the use of the aqualung. Various exercises are included to ensure that you gain confidence in the equipment and can readily orientate underwater. It takes some getting used to as your senses are much affected. You have no sense of smell and little taste. Colours fade as light is absorbed by the water. The only sounds are that of your used air bubbling out of the exhaust valve and a few odd noises from sea creatures or perhaps the movement of the tide on shingle. You learn to take responsibility for yourself and the care of your equipment. You also realise that you must be able to look after your buddy should he get into difficulties. When and where to dive is affected by the wind's effect on the water in the specific area so you also need to learn about the habits of the sea, tides, etc. You will also find out about the use of boats in relation to divers and other users of the sea.

The important thing when starting is to go at your own pace so that you can absorb all the information and become really proficient at the practical exercises. Do not get panic-stricken in the practical that you are getting left behind. In diving, as in all things, everyone is different. Some people are quicker to learn than others, or more agile. That does not mean they will necessarily be better divers in the long run. In fact, the opposite might possibly apply to some of them. Having learnt the basics with ease they become impatient for new experiences and end up in situations with which they are not equipped to cope.

Over-confidence is about the biggest hazard in diving as it leads you into all the dangers on the 'it won't happen to me' principle. However experienced you are you should always assume there is something you do not know. There are divers who go out with the intention of running risks. This sort of diver will take a boat out when everyone else stays in safe harbour. Someone then has to go to his aid when he gets into difficulties. He will dive beyond his own experience or capabilities, perhaps diving in deeper water or bad visibility. Risk takers can have a field day on a deep wreck. Entering a hold or hatchway without a guideline to his buddy outside, without a torch, without considering the possibility of fine silt rising in such clouds as to reduce visibility to nil. The disorientation resulting could prevent him from finding his way out again. Souvenir hunting with a hammer and chisel will make him use his air more quickly than leisurely sightseeing. This means an increased danger due to the necessity of conserving air for decompression. Running too low without being aware may mean having to carry out a free ascent. That in itself could lead to embolism (burst lung). If over the safe 'bottom' time it could even lead to the 'bends' (decompression sickness). This is a totally unnecessary risk to run during sport diving. All sensible sport divers operate with a reserve on the cylinder or a pressure gauge giving a guide to contents, and dive accordingly. Diving alone is not recommended.

Never let yourself be pushed into diving conditions about which you are not happy. For instance, if you are not happy diving at more than thirty metres then do not bother. It will be a waste of time and air as you will not remember anything worthwhile about the dive. Bad tension has a habit of distracting your attention from the life surrounding you. In some circumstances the opposite may apply in that being able to concentrate on something really fascinating may help you control your feelings. However, it is senseless to enter the water in a state of fear. A touch of normal apprehension is healthy and controllable, fear can lead to panic and possible disaster. Diving in any depth of water, however shallow, can be totally rewarding, just for the pleasure of being part of the flourishing environment. Just to be able to touch things you previously only saw in colour photographs or on television. To have schools of fish swim across the front of your mask and away with a flick of a hundred tails. To experience coming up through the water and, suddenly, back out into the air and sunlight once more.

All you need is the training and you too can spend time in that strange, wonderful world of colour and life. Treat it with respect and it will welcome you.

2
Physics Relating
to Diving

Some people wonder why it is vital they receive proper training before entering the sea with an aqualung. One of the reasons is that they must fully understand the laws which govern the way in which water pressure acts upon the body and upon the compressed air which we breathe. This chapter aims to explain these effects, as simply as possible. Diving is a practical sport. Once the theory is firmly lodged in your mind you can carry on and enjoy your diving.

We are entering a world where the atmosphere is entirely different from our own, one with no natural air supply. Our bodies are not designed to function in such a world and our senses are immediately affected. The sense of smell disappears, sound – if there is any noise at all – travels much faster underwater. Vision is affected.

Vision and light

Our visual sense reacts when light enters the eye and nerve impulses are sent to the brain where they are interpreted. Wearing a mask enables you to see underwater without your vision being blurred. However, objects will appear larger and closer than they really are, straight lines appear bent. This is caused by the light being 'refracted' on striking a water/air boundary, as it passes from the water through the glass into the air space between the mask and your eyes.

Light refraction

Refraction takes place when rays of light pass from the water to another medium, in this case air. Water is denser than air, therefore the rays of light are bent. Thus, when you look at an object the top of the object appears higher and the bottom lower. This causes it to appear larger and closer as shown in Fig 1. The distortion ratio is 3/4, ie if the object is 120cm away it will appear to be only 90cm.

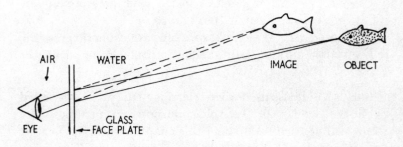

Fig 1 Effect of light refraction

Absorption

Absorption is a process whereby light is reduced in intensity by the water. White light, in this case from the sun, is made up of all colours. When passing through water a filtering process takes place. The first colour to disappear is red then, as you go deeper, yellow. Therefore, at depth most objects appear blue or green. Red objects can appear black.

Diffusion

Light underwater is deflected and scattered by the presence of particles suspended in the water.

The effects of pressure on the body and on compressed air

Atmospheric pressure

Atmospheric pressure is that pressure exerted on the body at sea level (14.7psi) by the weight of the atmosphere above. As you go further down below the sea this pressure increases. As you ascend it decreases.

Ambient pressure
This refers to the pressure immediately surrounding a diver. It is synonymous with absolute pressure.

Pressure is measured in two ways:

1 *Gauge pressure:* Most gauges register water pressure only, ie nil at the surface, 1atm at 10m and so on.
2 *Absolute pressure:* Water pressure plus atmospheric pressure, ie 1atm on the surface, 2atm at 10m, 3atm at 20m and so on (see Fig 2).

Bars is a unit also used when referring to the pressure exerted on the body and on air. To avoid confusion the unit atmosphere (atm) will be used throughout this chapter where applicable. An abbreviation for atmospheres sometimes used in diving books and magazines is ats instead of atm. Equipment now becoming available is more often marked in bars.

Boyles Law

Boyles Law states that if the pressure on a gas (air) is doubled, its volume is halved, but its density is doubled. Thus a cylinder full of air at the surface where the pressure is 1atm will be only half full at 10m and only a quarter full at 30m. As illustrated in Fig 2, it compresses by 50 per cent of its original volume in the first 10m but in the next 20m it only compresses another 25 per cent of its original volume. Therefore, compression of air under pressure is at its greatest near the surface. It decreases in intensity with depth. This explains why decompression stops after deep dives always take place within ten metres of the surface.

Although the volume decreases, the increased density of the air means that it contains the same number of usable

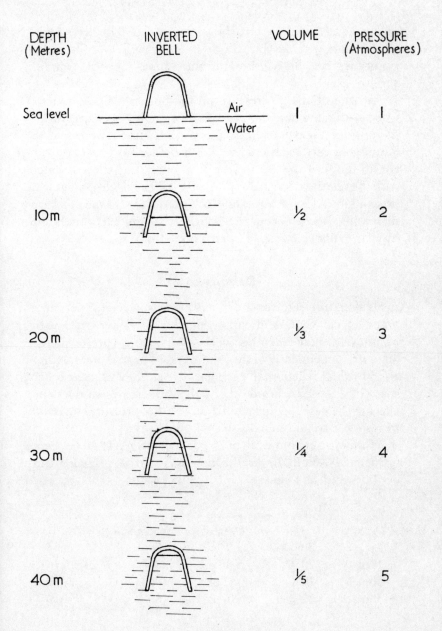

DEPTH (Metres)	INVERTED BELL	VOLUME	PRESSURE (Atmospheres)
Sea level	Air / Water	1	1
10m		½	2
20m		⅓	3
30m		¼	4
40m		⅕	5

Fig 2 Boyles Law

19

molecules. You will be breathing 'thicker' air. The deeper you go the more quickly you will breathe through your air, eg at twenty metres you will breathe three times more air than at surface level.

The alterations in pressure on the bottom will be noticed when swimming over the seabed. If swimming over a reef with its constant alterations in height, you may find it necessary to 'clear' your ears occasionally. This is because as you follow the rise in the reef up, you will be swimming in shallower water with the relative decrease in pressure. As the reef drops you will descend into deeper water and will therefore find the pressure increasing. It will, of course, be having the same effect on the air in your cylinder (see also burst lung on p 34).

Daltons Law

Air is a mixture of nitrogen (78.5 per cent) oxygen (21 per cent) argon (1 per cent) and carbon dioxide (0.03 per cent) with minute percentages of other inert gases. Each gas present in the air acts independently of the others and its partial pressure has an individual reaction, ie each gas acts entirely as if the other gases did not exist beside it. As depth increases so does the effect of the gases as their individual partial pressures increase in response to additional external pressure.

Assuming a relationship of 20 per cent oxygen to 80 per cent nitrogen present in the air, the increase in partial pressures can be illustrated as follows:

Depth	Oxygen	Partial pressure	Nitrogen	Partial pressure
0	20%	2.94 psi	80%	11.76 psi
10m	20%	5.88 psi	80%	23.52 psi
20m	20%	8.82 psi	80%	35.28 psi
30m	20%	11.76 psi	80%	47.04 psi

The small amounts of other constituents will also have increased their partial pressures but with very little effect. It is important to ensure that you have clean air. Traces of carbon monoxide at surface level are harmless, on a very deep dive they could increase in potency to a dangerous level.

Oxygen poisoning results from the increase in its partial pressure but this would only approach danger level at about forty-five metres so would not generally affect sport divers. It can occur during the use of an oxygen re-breather set. This equipment is generally considered too dangerous for use by sport divers but is used by some Navy divers. (See Decompression Sickness and Breathing Hazards pp 36–41.)

Charles Law

This states that 'if the pressure is kept constant, the volume of gas will vary directly with the absolute temperature'. This means that as the temperature of a gas rises or falls, the gas will also try to increase or decrease in volume. Cylinders have a fixed volume, therefore the gas inside is not allowed to expand or contract. Filled cylinders should be kept out of the hot sun.

During filling from a compressor some friction and the compression of air generates heat within the cylinder. The cylinder may feel quite warm to the touch. When it cools down there may be also a very slight drop in the pressure of the air within the cylinder. You may find that if a diving shop fills your bottle very quickly, when it has had time to cool the pressure in the cylinder will register less than full.

Archimedes Principle

This principle states that an object totally or partially submerged in a liquid will experience an upward force equal to the weight of liquid displaced. In the case of a diver underwater he will displace more water when his lungs are full of air than he will when he breathes out. On breathing in he will be positively buoyant as he will displace more water than his own bodyweight and he will rise. On breathing out he will be negatively buoyant and will sink as he will be displacing less water than his body weight. The ideal state of neutral buoyancy lies somewhere between the two.

To achieve neutral buoyancy it is necessary to go underwater wearing normal full diving equipment. By exhaling hard the diver will empty his lungs, reduce buoyancy and sink. By inhaling normally from the aqualung he increases buoyancy and rises. Adding or subtracting weights from the weightbelt during normal breathing rhythm he finally reaches a weight where he neither sinks nor rises.

Generally speaking it is easier to be slightly overweight when diving. Buoyancy is obviously affected by the equipment worn. A cylinder will be lighter when practically empty. At the end of a dive when near to the surface for decompression purposes the diver may find it very difficult to stay at the required depth but will find himself rising involuntarily. The suit also makes a difference as the air trapped inside will be compressed on sinking but buoyancy will be regained on ascent as the outside pressure lessens. Being too light means continually having to swim downwards particularly during a shallow dive and this can be extremely tiring.

Being slightly overweight can be counteracted by the use of air in the life-jacket and is the simplest way. However, it is a method which must be practised in the pool before use in the sea due to the dangers inherent in the practice. It is possible to control your buoyancy by breath control, to a certain extent, but there are also dangers in doing this and it should not be used to counteract an excessive over- or underweight condition.

Lifting objects

The cheapest way of lifting objects from the seabed is to use one or more large plastic containers (of the type used for washing-up liquid, etc). It can be taken underwater and attached by a line a few metres long to the object. Exhaled air from the aqualung is blown into the container. As it rises through the water and the outside pressure decreases, so the air will expand in the container. Any excess will flow out of the lower opening keeping the buoyancy at a constant level. Care has to be taken in using this method as, if the weight of the object is exceeded by the buoyancy of the container, its rate of ascent will increase rapidly. On surfacing the container may overturn completely, fill with water and begin to sink.

An alternative method is lifting bags. These can be bought or hired in different sizes, depending on the weight of the object you intend bringing to the surface. These generally, especially the larger ones, have exhaust valves on the top which allow the expanding air to escape at the surface. Here again, a too-rapid ascent can result in the bag folding over at the surface and spilling the air. If using one or more bag or container, it is important to watch what you are doing during filling, in case one end of the object starts to rise more quickly than the other.

3
Functions of the Human Body

The functions of the body depend on the availability of an external air supply which is affected by the increased pressure. The increasing pressure can also damage the cavities in the body and it is therefore important for a diver to understand how the body works and how its workings react under pressure.

The respiratory system

Breathing automatically provides the body with the oxygen it needs and removes the carbon dioxide which is a waste product. The body only holds enough oxygen in the red blood cells to last for approximately three minutes. After that cells in the brain become damaged and eventually death will occur.

Air passes from the nose and throat via the windpipe (trachea) which divides into two branches called bronchi; each bronchus sub-divides into a number of smaller branches known as bronchioles (see Fig 3). The ends of these are surrounded by tiny air sacs named alveoli. Each alveolus is covered by a network of capillaries. This is where the interchange of oxygen and waste (carbon dioxide) takes place.

The thorax is the chest cavity and this is completely filled with lungs, heart and large blood vessels. The connective tissue which binds together the blood vessels and airways has an elasticity which allows the lungs to expand or shrink as the chest cavity changes with each inspiration or exhalation of air.

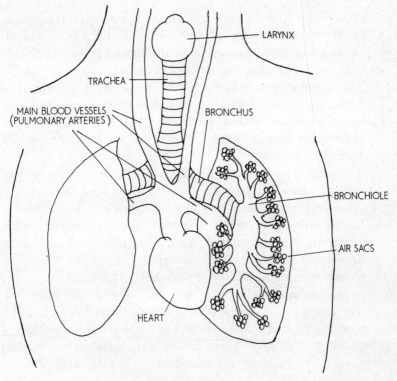

Fig 3 Lungs

The chest is lined with a membrane known as the pleura; another layer covers the surface of the lungs. A fluid between the two allows them to glide over each other without friction during breathing.

The bottom of the thorax is covered with a large layer of muscle, the diaphragm. The side walls are made up of ribs which are also covered with muscles. On inhaling, the diaphragm moves downward while the muscles of the chest walls lift the ribs upward and outward, thus increasing the size of the chest cavity. The air pressure within is therefore lowered and outside air rushes down the airways to inflate the air sacs at the end of each bronchiole. These inflated alveoli stretch the

25

lungs so that the extra lung space in the chest cavity is occupied. Exhaling causes the diaphragm to rise and the chest wall to contract downward squeezing out the air in the air sacs. The air sacs always hold a small amount of residual air.

During our breathing cycle oxygen and carbon dioxide is exchanged and this exchange allows us to oxygenate our tissues and remove some of the waste products. Air is made up of 21 per cent oxygen and only 0.03 per cent carbon dioxide. Normal expired air contains over 16 per cent oxygen and 4 per cent carbon dioxide. This shows that, while in the lungs, air has oxygen removed and replaced with carbon dioxide.

Air in the air sacs is separated from the blood in the capillaries by two very thin membranes. Immediately after inhalations these alveoli are high in oxygen pressure and low in carbon dioxide pressure. In the capillaries the blood has low oxygen pressure and high carbon dioxide pressure.

On reaching the tissues in other parts of the body the oxygenated blood releases oxygen from the red cells into the tissue fluid which is lower in oxygen content. From the fluids it passes into the cells to be used. Simultaneously, carbon dioxide moves in the opposite direction back to the lungs and thence is exhaled.

The whole cycle depends on the heart acting as an efficient pump to send oxygenated blood via the blood vessels from the lungs to the working tissues of the body.

Tidal volume

The air which passes through the lungs during one cycle of inspiration and expiration is known as the 'tidal volume'.

During exercise, the body demands more oxygen and has more carbon dioxide to dispel. The tidal volume must therefore be increased using the respiratory muscles. The maximum amount of gas we can exchange normally during a single breathing cycle is approximately 0.5 litre of air. A build-up of carbon dioxide in the body and a reduced oxygen level in the blood play their part in triggering the demand for more air.

The respiratory rate refers to the number of complete respiratory cycles taking place during one minute and this will vary according to the body's needs, whether resting or carrying out hard physical work.

The heart and bloodstream

The heart is situated behind the breastbone in the left front area of the chest. It is approximately the size of a clenched fist. Its function is to pump blood around the body and is made up mainly of muscular tissue. The left half collects blood returning from the lungs and pumps it through the circulatory system to the rest of the body. The right half collects the returning blood and sends it to the lungs. 'Non-return' valves ensure that the blood flows only in the correct direction (see Fig 4).

The average body contains approximately five litres of blood and this travels around the body transporting oxygen and carbon dioxide along an incredible network of arteries, veins and capillaries. The pressure at which the blood is pumped must stay within certain limits. If too low, a normal flow will

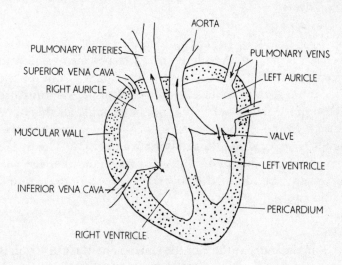

Fig 4 Heart

not be circulated to the tissues. If too high, the more delicate arteries might burst.

Red corpuscles in the blood carry oxygen. A smaller number of white cells, among other functions, help to fight infection. Plasma, the fluid of the blood, carries various substances, including nutrients, which help blood clotting in wounds. Oxygenated blood travels via the arteries. De-oxygenated blood returns to the heart via the veins. Arteries branch and re-branch many times and carry oxygen to the finest of individual cells.

Body tissues

Being mainly composed of water the tissues of the body can withstand enormous pressures. Four important tissues are the muscles, nervous tissues, bone, skin and mucous membranes. Excessive depth will not damage these tissues. However, the cavities of the body are always affected by pressure changes, especially when diving. Those most susceptible are sinuses, ears, lungs and the air passages to the lungs. The stomach may also be affected.

Sinuses

These are small air pockets lined with mucous membrane and connected with the nasal cavity. If the entry to any of the sinuses is blocked by mucus or tissue, air at normal pressure will be trapped inside and it will not be possible for this to be equalised. In this event a sharp pain will occur over the eye, along the nose, or above the teeth in the upper jaw. Unless the pressure can be equalised pain will persist and damage will occur, and the dive should therefore be abandoned immediately.

Mucous membranes

These line the inner surface of the sinuses and their function is to warm inspired air and catch germs, etc. With a cold, hayfever, etc, this membrane swells closing the opening to the sinuses and sinusitis may develop. No diving should be attempted when suffering from a heavy cold or other congestion. Some divers suffering from very slight congestion do make use of a nasal decongestant but this is not recommended.

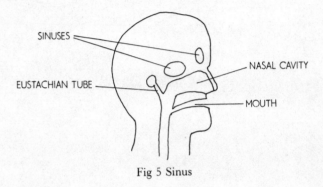

SINUSES

EUSTACHIAN TUBE

NASAL CAVITY

MOUTH

Fig 5 Sinus

The nose
This warms, moistens and cleanses the air as it passes on its way to the lungs. It is composed of bone and cartilage and is separated from the mouth by a bone partition called the hard palate. The bones of the face form the side walls. From each wall three ridges of bone extend into the nasal cavity and these increase the area through which air flows.

The ear
This is made up of several sections and is illustrated in Fig 6. The ear funnels sound into the outer ear canal. Glands in the walls of this canal secrete a wax (cerumen) which catches dust and other foreign objects which might damage the ear-drum. Ear infection in divers is sometimes caused by water-softened wax or bacteria in the canal. The canal slants inward and downward to the ear-drum (the delicate tympanic membrane). This separates the middle ear from the outer passage. On the other side of the ear-drum is the middle ear. This is filled with

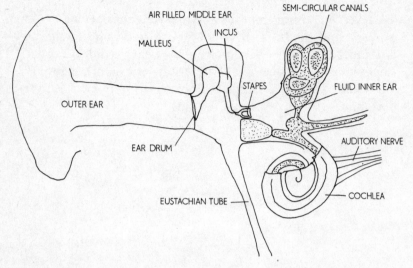

Fig 6 Ear

air. If the pressure of external water fluctuates greatly the drum will be forced to bulge inward or outward from the normal position. Excessive pressure on one side of the drum could cause a haemorrhage due to torn blood vessels, or even rupture the drum itself.

Equalisation of the pressures on the inner ear with those outside takes place by air passing through the eustachian tube which connects the middle ear with the throat. Again, if there is any blockage in this tube, then equalisation cannot take place. Ears should clear by 'popping' when pressure only is felt on the drums. A diver should not wait for pain. If this does occur he should ascend a small amount and try to clear (a metre or so). If impossible or pain persists, then he should return to the surface and abort the dive. Never blow excessively hard as you may force mucus into the inner ear.

Some divers always have to descend slowly being careful to clear before descending further and clearing again. Others have no problems and can clear just by swallowing hard and do not have to pinch their noses while snorting air downwards.

Another method is to wiggle the lower jaw from side to side and/or yawn (with mouth firmly clamped over mouthpiece). A tight-fitting rather than snug-fitting hood may contribute to problems and it may be necessary to pull the hood out slightly from each ear to allow water into the hood.

Teeth

Teeth should be kept in good condition. If they are neglected, an open cavity may provide a pocket to trap air at ambient pressure. A change in pressure during ascent or descent will affect the nerve of the tooth causing extreme pain.

The stomach

You will find that certain things eaten before diving affect you and this varies from diver to diver. Generally, anything which encourages the formation of gas in the stomach and intestines should be avoided for at least an hour or two before diving. There could be risk of cramp. 'Fizzy' drinks are bad, particularly some beers. In any case it is not advisable to take alcohol before diving. Salad ingredients, particularly onions and cucumber, can affect the stomach. Chewing gum during a dive is definitely not recommended. Neither should you enter the water with a stomach grumbling with hunger. Most liquids – tea, coffee, milk and soup – seem to suit the majority as do bread in moderation, dairy products and meat (only if not highly spiced).

Bear in mind too that if you are diving from a boat you may be affected by certain types of water movement, eg a gentle swell, short chop, etc. Try and save your large food intake for after the dive.

4
General Fitness and Hazards Involved

General fitness

Generally speaking, anyone of average fitness will be safe to dive. You should have a medical before doing so, preferably with a doctor having special knowledge of diving requirements. If not, your local doctor will be prepared to carry out an examination paying particular attention to ears, sinuses, lungs, heart and blood pressure.

Diving puts extra strain on the heart and lungs. If you have a serious weight problem you are already putting strain on these organs. Probably you will be advised to deal with your weight before commencing training with the aqualung.

Abnormally high blood pressure which has to be treated by drugs will stop you from diving. Anyone suffering from an illness or disability which requires the regular use of drugs may find himself barred from diving. Heart trouble, diabetes or asthma cases must have their individual complaints thoroughly investigated by a medical practitioner before commencing training. Any condition in a person which could lead to their becoming unconscious underwater should not dive. Anyone with epilepsy in their history is considered unsafe for diving.

Also affected by pressure are the stomach and teeth. In addition to your medical check-up, regular dental checks should be made. Have any bad teeth or loose fillings put in order. If you wear full dentures or partial dentures, make sure they are well fitted and firmly fixed if you intend to wear them underwater.

Temporary unfitness for diving can be caused by any infection of the ears, lungs and nasal cavities, eg colds, catarrh, bronchitis, hayfever, otitis media (inflamed eardrum) and others.

Alcohol should never be taken before diving. Likewise a hangover leaves you less fit than you should be. Sedatives and even some types of seasickness tablets may affect the body for up to twenty-four hours, so care must be exercised in the choice and use of such tablets.

We have seen that water exerts increasing pressure on the body with depth. The body becomes almost weightless. The mask enables you to see with clear vision underwater but, due to the refractive effect of water on light, objects appear to be closer and larger than is the case.

One thing to bear in mind is that we are thinking animals blessed with imagination. This can, occasionally, produce over-reaction to something underwater which would have no effect on land. Entering a completely strange environment, encumbered by various pieces of equipment immediately puts you at a disadvantage in the first stages of training. Soon you adjust to this and it ceases to affect you.

If you are a chronic sufferer from claustrophobia on land then probably nothing will induce you to try diving. Mild sufferers can and do dive. You may just have to limit yourself in the type of diving you do. For instance, exceptionally poor visibility may affect you. However, this will not interfere with your enjoyment, most divers have a particular thing with which they are not totally at home. The field is so large that there are plenty of other avenues to follow.

By the time you have finished reading this chapter it is hoped that you will be convinced that diving is a sport which needs thorough prior training from experienced instructors. It is not the sort of sport where you can learn what you need to know from a book and then go happily out, buy the equipment and carry on diving regardless of consequences. There are numerous hazards, both major and minor, involved in diving which are detailed below. However, it should be emphasised that, with the proper training, these dangers can almost always be avoided. Thousands of sensible people dive year after year without mishap.

Exhaustion

Mental and/or physical exhaustion are caused by doing too much. A sensible diver learns to recognise his own limits. There is a difference between the fatigue which will be put right by a good night's sleep and the totally drained feeling which is still with you when you crawl out of bed in the morning. In that state you do not dive. If you overestimate your fitness then you must do all you can to conserve energy. Signal to your buddy that you are out of breath and wish to slow down (see Fig 21). Alternatively, signal that you wish to change direction and swim with the tide rather than against it. A deep dive will make matters far worse as the deeper you go the more work your body has to do just to get enough air, so stay in fairly shallow water (say, under twenty to twenty-two metres). Do not endanger your own safety or that of your buddy by trying to continue the dive when you know you are not fit enough. Signal that you are 'dodgy' and wish to ascend and he will accompany you to the surface.

On the surface rest on your inflated life-jacket. If you really feel capable of doing so then signal you are OK and swim in a leisurely fashion to the boat, if it is an anchored boat (if an inflatable or similar unanchored then it can pick you up). If you are exhausted give the distress signal to the boat and rest on your life-jacket until it comes to pick you up.

Burst lung

A burst lung occurs if the pressure of air within the lungs rises in relation to external pressures. Once the air in the lungs has increased its pressure over the pressure exerted outside the body, the lung will have reached the point where maximum stretch has been exceeded. The result will be that the lung will have to rupture as it will be unable to contain the air being held inside it.

The lungs will hold six litres of air. Even if you completely emptied your lungs, ie breathed out as hard as possible, there would still be a residual amount of air of one and a half litres in your lungs. If you did this at, say, thirty metres, this small amount of air would expand in volume as the external pressure decreased on ascent. By the time you reached the surface your lungs would be full. Any lessening in external pressure can increase the volume of air in your lungs. Even ascending only a few metres while holding the breath can increase the possibility of a burst lung, eg during training in a swimming-pool. The more shallow the water becomes, the more the risk will increase, due to the increased lessening of pressure and the relative increase in the build-up of the air pressure in the lungs (see Boyles Law on p 18).

The demand valve is so designed as to adjust automatically to the changing pressure of the water. Therefore, you are supplied with air to keep your lungs at the same pressure as that outside your body. As long as you breathe regularly there is no danger. Problems arise if you hold your breath on ascent, or if you surface more quickly than the normal safe ascent rate. This rate is approximately twenty metres a minute or at the rate of the small bubbles which are rising above you. The risks involved in either of these situations are as follows.

Air embolism
When air from the ruptured lung finds its way into the circulation bubbles of air form in the blood system where they become lodged. Supplies of blood and therefore oxygen are prevented from being carried beyond that point. A heart attack could result if the supply to the heart muscle is blocked. Lack of

oxygen supply to the brain can result in brain damage or death unless recompression takes place immediately. Other parts of the body can be affected to a greater or lesser degree ranging from giddiness and defects in speech and vision, to partial paralysis of limbs.

Spontaneous pneumothorax
This occurs if air bursts through the rupture and lodges in the pleural cavity (between the lungs and the chest wall). The expansion of this trapped air could possibly collapse the lung. Chest pains, coughing or shortness of breath could be warning signs. Immediate recompression and medical treatment are essential.

Interstitial emphysema
This is caused by air getting into the tissues within the chest cavity. It may spread under the skin at the base of the neck. Symptoms are similar to those in pneumothorax. Recompression may be required.

Decompression sickness

A descending diver absorbs nitrogen in greater amounts than on the surface, due to the increased pressure of the surrounding water and the action of this pressure on the partial pressures of the constituents of the air he is breathing (see Daltons Law on p 19). This increased intake of nitrogen must be allowed to dissipate in the body naturally, through the normal course of respiration. It is vital to be aware of the depth and duration of the dive. Even relatively shallow water (say twenty metres) can produce the bends in a diver if he stays down longer than the recommended time and fails to carry out the necessary decompression stops according to the decompression tables (see p 38). If he should swim direct to the surface in these conditions then the excess nitrogen will form bubbles in the bloodstream and these bubbles will move to the joints.

Symptoms do not normally appear immediately, a delay of up to an hour can be experienced.

The bends
The most common form of the sickness. These are pains mainly in and around the joints or deep in the muscles. These pains range from mild aches to unbearable pain.

The niggles
The mild aches in joints and muscles usually disappear and are generally ignored by divers. Any increase in intensity of the pain should be dealt with immediately.

Skin bends
Another mild form of sickness is the skin bend. This takes the form of rashes which can appear anywhere on the body. On its own a skin bend can safely be ignored but is a sign that insufficient decompression has been carried out. A warning, as are the niggles, for greater care in planning the next dive.

Serious effects
When the sickness affects the nervous system or respiratory system then the situation is extremely serious. Symptoms are weakness of muscles or paralysis. Pins and needles sensation in extremities. Deafness or impaired vision. If the brain is affected the diver may go into convulsions, experience nausea and vomit, suffer slurred speech and become paralysed. He may lose consciousness.

If the respiratory system is impaired he may suffer from the 'chokes'. Shortly after a dive the victim finds it extremely difficult to breathe. This is combined with a tight feeling across the chest. It is a form rarely seen but is extremely serious and requires immediate treatment to avoid fatality.

Each case of decompression sickness must be treated on its symptoms in the individual and must be treated by medical care and recompression. The possible exception are the niggles or rashes, fading after a short time but these must be watched to ensure the condition does not worsen. Decompression sickness will more readily affect an obese diver or one who is already exhausted and run down through, say, overwork.

To ensure safe diving in this respect it is essential that all dives are planned as to time and depth. Deep dives are particularly hazardous and there should be strict observation of tables and stops. No novice diver should attempt dives which will require decompression stops unless accompanied by an experienced diver, preferably an instructor. He should also have been diving regularly over the preceding period, gradually increasing depths, before doing so.

Decompression tables
These can be purchased at diving shops or obtained through diving clubs or associations and should be studied by all divers. These tables do vary according to the country of origin. Obviously wherever you dive in the world you will prefer to continue with the tables in whose use you have been trained. They must be consulted before entering the water to ensure both divers agree on the bottom time they intend to allow and what length of stops will be necessary. This includes more shallow dives which may not need stops. Tables are available printed on rigid plastic and these can be attached to the life-jacket so that they are not mislaid. They are also produced in a plastic material which will adhere to the arm of a diving suit. However, this does not mean the diver should wait until he is underwater before consulting them, they just provide a safety check. Having consulted tables, calculated times and stops, both divers must synchronise watches to avoid confusion underwater.

The tables give duration of dives at each depth allowed without carrying out a decompression stop or stops. They also give various times and the stops necessary. They assist in calculating times should it be intended to carry out two dives in one day. In this case the times of both dives are combined and decompression is carried out at stops relevant to the depth of the deepest dive. Obviously, of the two dives the more shallow of them should be carried out second.

Breathing hazards

Oxygen poisoning

This is caused by breathing excessive amounts of oxygen. The possibility of a sport diver suffering from such a thing is practically nil as the partial pressure of the oxygen will not approach danger level until a depth of around forty-five metres. The use of oxygen re-breathers is banned for sport divers. They are used by the Navy only in less than ten metres.

Nitrogen narcosis

This, generally speaking, does not affect a diver until he is in at least thirty metres and then it is a fairly rare occurrence. The effects vary from diver to diver but the dangers should not be minimised. It has a similar effect to that of too much alcohol or the effect of drugs. The diver becomes over-confident, his surroundings become unreal and he is unable to concentrate or make decisions. In extreme cases he suffers hallucinations and disorientation. These symptoms can attack within minutes.

This state can affect novice divers; more often it is connected with those divers suffering from a hangover, overwork, or some seasickness tablets have been blamed for increasing the possibility of narcosis.

Suspected subjects should immediately be brought to shallower water or to the surface. Luckily there is immediate relief from the symptoms and no after-effects are suffered. Subjects often, as with alcohol, do not remember what has happened during their 'trip'.

Hypoxia and anoxia

Hypoxia is, simply, a lack of oxygen, whereas anoxia is a state of total absence of oxygen. Hypoxia is a condition where the tissues of the body receive insufficient oxygen or are unable to use the oxygen received. It could happen in the event of the mouthpiece being knocked out of the mouth, air failing to come through on demand, or a foreign body in the mouth causing obstruction to air flow. Symptoms of the hypoxic state occur without warning and generally are loss of concentration, emotional instability, confusion, loss of muscle control, impaired nervous system leading to unconsciousness and death in extreme cases. In the case of hypoxia, air or oxygen should be administered immediately plus medical treatment. Lack of oxygen to the brain can cause irreparable damage within a maximum of four minutes, followed by death.

Carbon monoxide poisoning

Air in the cylinder can be contaminated by this gas in two ways. The filters of the compressor may not be functioning correctly or the air intake may be contaminated by the fumes of an engine. The second is a good reason for not using a portable compressor in a busy car park. It is a tasteless and odourless gas but some air may be 'tasty' if contaminated with it.

Symptoms are headache, nausea, dizziness and weakness, and the fingernails and lips may be cherry red. Unconsciousness can occur without prior warning in extreme cases. Artificial respiration must be given if breathing has stopped; mild cases should still receive medical attention.

Carbon dioxide

Air normally contains approximately 0.03 per cent carbon dioxide. If the breath is held, as in snorkelling, the partial pressure of carbon dioxide rises as the partial pressure of oxygen falls. The brain is thus stimulated to ask for air to dispel this excess carbon dioxide.

During snorkel diving, hyperventilation is a dangerous practice which increases the duration of breath-holding. It involves taking a number of rapid deep breaths and forced exhalations prior to diving. It is dangerous because it reduces the carbon dioxide content and at the same time reduces the desire to breathe. This lack of desire to breathe can lead to hypoxia and even loss of consciousness underwater. *Never* take more than four deep breaths, when snorkelling, before diving each time.

Carbon dioxide excess can also be caused by incorrect breathing. Deep gasps of compressed air taken in, followed by small exhalations, can lead to a build-up of carbon dioxide during diving with an aqualung.

Carbon dioxide excess gives rise to laboured breathing, possibly headaches, dizziness, weakness and often nausea. In extreme cases the diver may lose consciousness. Generally these cases will revive satisfactorily when given fresh air, artificial respiration or, if essential, oxygen.

Other hazards

Hypothermia
This is a lowering of the body temperature. In diving, this is due to loss of body heat as a result of a poorly fitting suit or a suit too thin for the conditions in which you are diving. At first you will feel merely cold – that is the time to come up. Therefore, signal to your buddy by simulating shivering and follow this by the ascent signal. It is not only stupid but dangerous to continue after the first warning signs. As the condition worsens your brain ceases to function clearly, your head is muzzy and the smallest decision seems impossible. Your chilled limbs become at first as heavy as lead. Eventually you feel as though you are not moving at all, worse still, it does not seem to matter. To take it to extremes, hypothermia can lead to coma and death. Should you start to shiver, surface; you will not enjoy diving with chattering teeth in any case as you will not be able to concentrate enough to register anything.

Back on the boat or land, immediately put on a windproof jacket or oilskins. If it is a long boat trip then all the divers should be carrying windproof jackets to put on over suits. Better still, dry and dress straight away if possible. Take a drink, preferably a warm one and definitely not alcoholic. A bad case of hypothermia should be put out of the wind. If the boat is small then he should be laid in the bottom of the boat covered with oilskins or, preferably, a survival blanket. Where there is room another body should lie down with the casualty under the coverings to help prevent further loss of body heat. Medical attention should be sought as soon as possible.

Seasickness

Seasickness can attack in different conditions of sea, either in the boat or just on the surface of the sea, eg while holding on to the side of the cover boat. Do not bother to try and cover up your condition. A big percentage of regular boat users suffer at some time or another.

It can attack a diver once the boat has stopped and he is kitting up. If you are so affected then, if space permits, get ready as far as possible on your way to the dive site. On reaching it you can then drop into the water if conditions allow, and wait for your buddy on the surface holding on to a line to the boat.

Very slight nausea in some divers can disappear as soon as they are in the water. Real cases of seasickness, particularly with vomiting and fatigue, mean that the sufferer should not dive. Any possibility of vomiting underwater is extremely dangerous. As in all other situations, the rule is when in doubt, do not dive. You may be putting someone else at risk as well as yourself.

Ear squeeze

This is caused by the increased pressure on the drum through the outer ear, during descent. It can be avoided easily by equalising the pressure. Pinch the nostrils and blow down the nose until the ears 'pop', or use one of the other methods which suits you. Equalise as the pressure builds up, do not wait until pain is experienced. If it is, ascend a short distance until the pain ceases and equalise at that point. Try going down again and equalise as necessary. If you descend ignoring both pressure and pain the pressure will build up to such an extent that the drum will rupture. Some bleeding will probably be noted on return to the surface. Underwater the cold water entering the inner ear through the ruptured drum could cause loss of balance so that you spin around.

Should you rupture an ear-drum seek medical attention immediately to avoid any infection setting in. No amateur doctoring with branded goods should take place. The drum, with medication, should heal gradually on its own in a matter of a few weeks. If lucky you should be diving again within three months. This varies and bad cases may require surgery or even prevent further diving.

Diving with a cold, hayfever, or similar congestion can interfere with the equalising of pressure.

Sinus squeeze

Colds, hayfever, or other allergy, can cause the opening to the sinuses to block. This is due to swelling of the mucous membrane lining the sinuses and nasal passages. It leads to intense pain across the forehead and/or under the eyes during descent. In this event, surface. Rupture of a mucous membrane in the sinus cavity usually leads to a discharge of blood and mucus. Decongestants are not recommended although some divers use them after surfacing, not before a dive.

Mask squeeze

A suction-like effect created in the mask caused by failure to exhale very slightly through the nose on descent to equalise pressure, or by unwittingly inhaling through the nose at some stage during descent.

In bad cases it may result in haemorrhage of small blood vessels in the face and eyes. The areas around the eyes may be swollen and bruised and the whites of the eyes reddened.

If the mask begins to feel tight on descent simply exhale gently through the nose into the mask to equalise the pressure; if the mask was fitted correctly at the surface this will be sufficient. Should it continue, ascend about a metre and again try equalising by exhaling into the mask through the nose. If this does not help return to the surface. You may find it necessary to return to the boat and refit the mask.

Hood squeeze
This will normally only take place if the hood you are wearing is too small and tight for you. Should the hood start to exert too much pressure on descent, allowing water into it should help. An easy method is to put the forearm over the top of the head from back to front and press down. This will produce small gaps on either side of the forehead without interfering with the fit of the mask. Water will then enter the hood.

5
Snorkelling Equipment and Techniques

Snorkelling equipment

Before going into the sea with an aqualung it is necessary to become proficient in the sport of snorkelling which will bring you some of the basic skills also used in scuba diving. It will build confidence in the water, coupled with a respect for the changing moods of the sea. What can be seen underwater while just holding your breath is unbelievable. It will give you a foretaste of the fascinating world you will be able to visit with an aqualung.

The basic equipment needed for snorkelling are mask, snorkel and fins (see Fig 7). However, a life-jacket and a diving float or buoy, also a diver's knife are desirable. If diving in cold waters such as around Britain then a wetsuit is an essential at any time of the year. Because of its buoyancy a weightbelt will also be necessary. It is important to buy any gear from a proper diving shop where they are able to give you help and advice. Never make false economies buying cheap 'plastic' gear designed for the holiday trade.

Face mask
By providing an air space between your eyes and the water, the mask allows you to see as clearly as you can in the air. However, there is a distortion which makes objects appear larger and closer than they really are. The mask should always give a

45

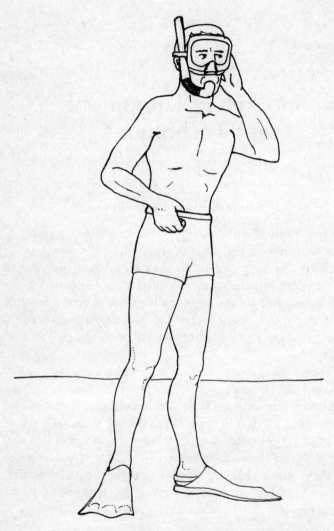

Fig 7 Snorkeller kitted up with mask, snorkel and fins

comfortable watertight seal. If too tight, it could cause a headache, if too loose, it will leak. Test the mask by placing it in position on your face and inhale gently through the nose. If it does not form a suction, air is entering and it will leak underwater.

The lens must be either tempered or safety glass. Plastic lenses tend to mist up underwater and scratch easily. Plain glass lenses would be too prone to breakage for safety. If you have to wear glasses all the time on land you may wish to arrange for suitable lenses to be fitted into a mask. This is, of course, a specialist task, but it is possible to find an optical works able and prepared to carry out this work for you.

Recesses on either side of the nose enable the nose to be pinched from outside the mask to facilitate ear clearing and are essential. During training you will be shown how to clear water from a mask with ease. Masks are made with purge valves in the glass or in the rubber which allow water to be expelled from the mask without it having to be removed or the seal with the face broken. A properly fitted mask rarely floods but it is good for the confidence of the diver to know he can cope with such an eventuality so the mask-clearing training is an essential part of the course.

Fins

Fins move you through the water with ease. Underwater they enable you to swim without the use of arms leaving your hands free.

Here again, it is a matter of personal choice but comfort is more important than design. A loose fin will cause chafing and may even come off underwater which could be dangerous. A tight fin may cause cramp. Remember you will be wearing them with a wetsuit so you should try on your fins over a neoprene boot – unless you habitually dive in warm waters where a wetsuit is not necessary. Most divers start out with the basic type of fin but, as they become stronger in the leg and more experienced, they change to the giant or jet type of fin.

Snorkels

Snorkels are 'J'–shaped tubes with a mouthpiece. They enable you to keep your face in the water beneath you and this can be a real advantage when swimming on the surface, over long distances, perhaps back to a boat or the shore after completing an aqualung dive. It allows you to keep your eyes on the bottom or relax motionless on the surface to rest. You can submerge to adjust equipment, tie lines, etc.

Water will fill an open snorkel when you are submerged. This can be blown out on the surface with a short, forceful exhalation. Attempts to produce an underwater breathing tube extending from the diver on the bottom, up to the surface, met with failure. The weight of only thirty centimetres of water exerts such pressure against the body that it requires a terrific effort to inflate the lungs against it. At only a metre or so depth the pressure is so great that inflating the lungs in order to inhale through the snorkel becomes impossible. This is the reason why they are only used for surface breathing.

There are several different types on the market but a simple 'J' type with not too long a tube is best. The diameter should be large enough not to interfere with easy breathing but not so large as to make clearing it difficult. To prevent the snorkel from being lost it should be attached to the strap of the mask by a band of rubber. It can be worn tucked under the strap of the mask but this is not totally satisfactory. It is not as comfortable, nor as safe. A snorkel is an essential, not an accessory, particularly if you find yourself on the surface in a choppy sea with very little air in your cylinder.

Snorkelling techniques

It is assumed that you can already swim before you consider learning to dive. If joining a club you will be required to pass a swimming test before you are accepted as a trainee member. This will probably include swimming several lengths of a pool freestyle and backstroke, followed by swimming a specified distance wearing a weighted belt. Treading water, floating and retrieving objects from the bottom of the pool is also included. All this takes place, naturally, without the aid of mask and fins. The test is designed to assess not only your swimming ability but your stamina, confidence in the water, and perseverance.

If learning through a school they will probably not be as particular with regard to your swimming proficiency. However, for your own sake it is desirable that you should work at improving your swimming. This will keep you fit as well as making you more competent in the water.

Before going into the sea with any equipment you will spend some time in a swimming-pool getting used to various aspects of its use. Alternatively you may start your snorkel training in a shallow area in the sea.

To prevent the mask from misting up, spit in the mask and rub the saliva over the glass, rinsing it afterwards in the pool. Adjust the mask for a comfortable airtight fit. Make sure that all your hair is pushed back from your face with one hand before fitting the mask over your eyes and nose with the other. Even one strand of hair under the rubber will break the seal enough to allow water to enter. Breathe in through the nose; if it does not form a suction, air is entering and it will leak.

Once the mask is comfortable, slip the tube of the snorkel under the strap, unless it is already attached to it with a band. Putting the mouthpiece in your mouth, adjust the snorkel until it is comfortable then, standing in the pool, put your face into the water. If you put your head in too far water will rush into your mouth through the snorkel. Try to look forward and down, not straight down. After a bit of practice you will know when you have altered your head position to the wrong angle.

Now move further up the pool. Practise dipping the snorkel underwater and blowing the water out with short sharp puffs. Keep your lips firmly around the mouthpiece but try not to clench it with your teeth. This is not necessary and just makes your jaws ache. The main thing to remember is to remain relaxed. Tension wastes energy. Swim in the pool until you are quite happy with the mask – some people suffer from a 'suffocating' feeling but this quickly disappears as you get accustomed to breathing through your mouth.

With your fins on, swim in a leisurely fashion, using the crawl kick but letting the knees bend slightly and pointing the toes, trying not to break the water with the fins. Most of the work should be done by the thigh muscles rather than by the leg and ankle. Practise until you move easily, without effort, and without loads of splashing. Keep your arms by your sides while finning or clasp your hands behind your back. You will find that dipping the fins in the water before putting them on helps in fitting them, particularly when wearing neoprene boots.

Learn to let the water support you. Remove your mask and float on the surface face downwards, breathing through the snorkel. Try swimming on the surface, again using the snorkel only, this accustoms you to water on your face. Tread water while putting on and removing your mask several times. Clear the water from the mask by looking up towards the roof and tipping the bottom away from your face. You cannot use the leg action normally employed while treading water. Instead, use your normal finning stroke, staying upright, trying to keep your legs from bending too much. It seems odd at first but is simple and effective.

Duck diving

To take you to the bottom of the sea or pool you need to be able to 'duck dive'. From a prone position on the surface, reach your arms and trunk as deep as possible, as if trying to touch your knees with your head. At the same time lift your feet over your head, pulling downwards strongly with your arms. Swim underwater keeping the same finning stroke as used on the surface. Do not use your arms. Try to make your strokes longer. You should feel that your legs are moving in sweeping strokes from the hips. This is illustrated in Fig 8.

Before duck diving, take a breath through your snorkel just before you submerge. It is not necessary to fill the lungs. In fact,

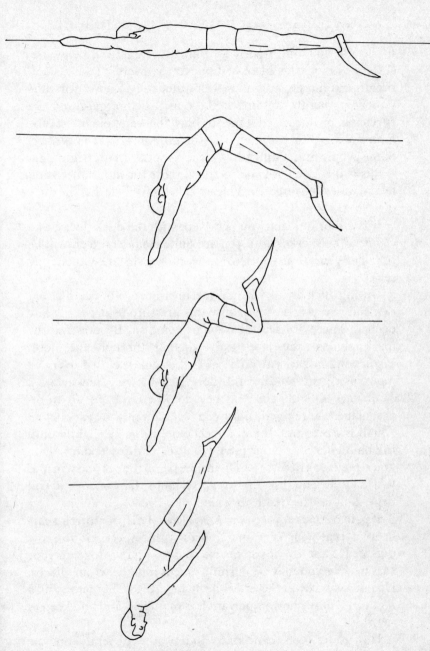

Fig 8 Duck diving

if you do, you will experience difficulty in getting below the surface due to your increased buoyancy. Merely take a small breath, submerge, and allow the water to run down the tube into your mouth, holding it there as if before gargling. On surfacing, having saved some air, blow the water out of the tube with a sharp puff and then carry on swimming on the surface. Some people find it difficult to clear a snorkel in the beginning. If this is the case with you merely remove the mouthpiece and let the water run out. Concentrate at first on mastering the duck dive.

It is important that you persevere with the duck diving and clearing the snorkel until you are quite confident. You will be thankful you did if you have to swim any distance in choppy seas.

During duck diving you may feel pressure on your ears as you descend and you must equalise this pressure before going any deeper. There are several ways of doing so. By pressing the mask against the face and exhaling through the nose; swallowing hard; 'yawning' with the mouth closed over the mouthpiece, or holding the nose and blowing downwards. Your ears should 'pop' as they do when you go up in an aeroplane. Do not wait until you feel pain in your ears before equalising pressure. If you do feel pain, come up slightly until the pain goes away and then equalise. Try descending again and equalise as necessary. Diving deeper in the sea you will find you have to equalise the pressure more than once – it will depend upon the depth to which you dive.

If pain persists *do not go any deeper*. Do not risk bursting an eardrum. Treat your ears and sinuses with respect. Go to see a doctor. Do not dive if you have a cold – if you try to force your ears to clear you may be pushing mucus into the wrong places. Do not wear earplugs ever, while diving. Read Chapters 2 and 3 and you will see how important it is to understand and keep to the rules.

How long you can stay underwater depends on the individual and his experience. Moving slowly and in a relaxed manner helps you to stay down longer. Something you must not do in your attempts to stay down longer and deeper is to boost the amount of air in your lungs before diving. Never take more than four deep breaths before a duck dive. Hyperventilation, as it is known, involves taking a number of very deep breaths and forced exhalations before submerging. This has the effect of flushing some of the carbon dioxide out of your system. Without this carbon dioxide you will not feel the same desire to breathe when the oxygen supply becomes very low in your body. This can lead to unconsciousness underwater.

To help build confidence and stamina there are some exercises carried out in training. These can be performed regularly to keep fit even after you have gone on to become an experienced aqualung diver.

Retrieving equipment
Tread water on the surface, remove fins, mask and snorkel. Allow them to drop to the bottom of the pool. Tread water to assess their position. Dive for mask, surface and refit while treading water. Dive for fins, one at a time, fitting while treading water.

Forward and backward rolls
Forward rolls are simple, being basically a somersault underwater. Swim along the surface of the water then duck dive underneath, using your arms to help you. Tuck your head and arms in and bend your knees so that you go into a ball. You will find that you somersault quite naturally.

The backward roll sometimes requires a little more practice and you approach it in the same way. Diving down almost to the bottom of the pool, you then point yourself back up again in the direction of the surface. Use your arms in a circular clockwise motion. At the same time tilt your head well back and arch your body. Keep your legs still and fairly close together. Concentrate on the actions, do not try to look at the direction in which you are going, this often sends you off course. The correct

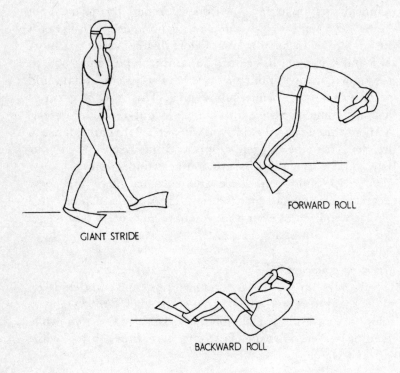

GIANT STRIDE

FORWARD ROLL

BACKWARD ROLL

Fig 9 Methods of pool entry

result should be a backward somersault. These rolls are a very good exercise in accustoming you to the effects of disorientation underwater, and helping you in recovering from them quickly. The water entry exercises are also worth practising for this reason, particularly the backward roll.

Methods of pool entry

There are various forms of entry into the water of which there are three in most general use (see Fig 9). Make sure the water is clear below you before you enter, ie there are no divers, swimmers, or other obstructions.

Giant stride

Stand on the side of the pool, feet on the edge, fins overhanging. Place one hand over mask (if you lost it going into the sea you could be in trouble), the other arm by your side. Lean slightly forward, take a large step out and down into the water, turning slightly as you do so. Alternatively, if the height above the water is higher than, say, the normal height of the side of the pool above the water, then it is best to enter the water with feet together, one fin slightly over the other.

Forward roll

Stand on the edge of the pool as before. Slightly bend the knees and bend at the waist, both hands on your mask. Continue bending forward at the waist and knees tucking your head in until you roll forwards into the water. You will surface right side up.

Backward roll

Stand on the edge with your heels over the side and facing away from the water. Make sure the area is clear, hold the mask in place as before with both hands. Bend the legs, tuck head into chest and then roll backwards as though sitting on air. You will not go far beneath the surface and will bob up like a cork immediately. Remember, in both the rolling entries, to tuck the head well in and bend the knees. The rest of the body will follow correctly.

When practising these entries in snorkelling gear only, remember to take a small breath before entering the water.

Remember

1 When using the pool for training stay aware of what other pool users are doing, they may not see you underwater.
2 When entering the water always hold on to your mask.
3 When snorkelling in deeper water your mask may start to press hard on your face. A snort of air through your nose into your mask will equalise the pressure.

4 Never continue a descent if you are unable to equalise the pressure on your ears.
5 Never indulge in breath-holding contests to see who can swim the farthest underwater. Diving, for the sake of safety, must remain a non-competitive sport.
6 Never hyperventilate.

6
Life-saving

General

If you see someone in trouble in the water naturally you want to help them. It is important that you should not in turn get into trouble and add to the problems. Assess the situation quickly in relation to your own ability.

Never swim out to rescue someone where an alternative is available. In a river it may be possible to use a branch, towel or jacket to extend your reach while lying full length on the bank. If not there may be an object which will float such as a ball, empty polythene container, etc, which you can throw out to the casualty to give support. It may be possible to wade part-way out into the river, making sure you do not get taken by the current yourself. If there are several rescuers, extend your reach by forming a human chain. Whatever attempt is being made *always talk to the casualty* to give him encouragement.

Never attempt to swim out to effect a rescue if you can commandeer a boat and arrive more quickly, at less risk to yourself. It also increases the chances of survival for the casualty – assuming he is conscious and can hold on to the stern of the dinghy. If accompanied, you may be able to get him aboard.

If you are a snorkel or aqualung diver then it is important for you to learn some basic methods of recovering someone in trouble and of giving expired air resuscitation (EAR) on land or on the surface. The following will give you an outline of the seriousness of what is involved. It will give you basic methods to practise. As a regular water user you should attempt to get some formal training. A good standard can normally be acquired through a diving club or swimming club.

Techniques

Having seen another diver in trouble you must swim to him arriving in a fit state to cope, not out of breath. Use an overarm stroke so that you can keep your face out of the water and watch the victim the whole time. He may go under in which case you need to see the exact spot in the hope of arriving in time to retrieve him from underwater. Assuming he is on the surface, approach him from behind, talk to him to calm him down, and grasp him with confidence, again from behind and to his left side. Immediately he is calm enough, tow him to the shore or boat using the following method.

1 With the left hand grip the upper left arm.
2 With the right hand cup his chin in the palm with the thumb sealing the mouth.

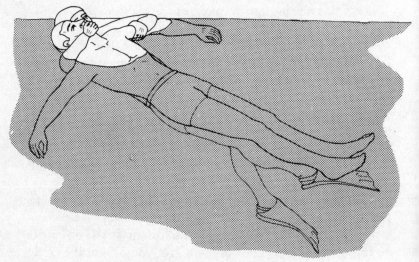

Fig 10 Close up arm tow

58

TILT HEAD AND LIFT JAW

ENSURE THE AIR PASSAGES
ARE CLEAR

CLOSE MOUTH FOR MOUTH
TO NOSE RESUSCITATION

MAINTAIN TILT OF HEAD FOR
MOUTH TO MOUTH RESUSCITATION

PINCH NOSE AND COMMENCE
INFLATION

Fig 11 Expired air resuscitation (EAR)

3 Right forearm should bear lightly over subject's right
   shoulder during towing.
4 Fin steadily.

This method known as the Close Up Arm Tow and illustrated
in Fig 10 can be used on swimmers and divers alike and can be
adapted to use on approaching the subject from his right side. It

can be used for towing someone suffering from cramp or fatigue or can be adapted to use on someone requiring EAR on the surface.

If the subject is obviously drowning then EAR must be given immediately. Fig 11 shows the alternative methods. If he is a full-kitted diver then you will inflate his life-jacket sufficiently to keep him afloat on his back should you be forced by circumstances to lose contact with him momentarily. Do not inflate it too much as this will impede your efforts to give EAR and will increase difficulty in eventual towing. Discard your own weightbelt to increase your buoyancy as it will not be possible to use your own life-jacket inflated. Likewise, if the tow is likely to be a long one it may be necessary to ditch your aqualung set also as it will impede your progress when towing.

Approach the subject from behind to his left side. If he is face down turn him over. Remove his mask, snorkel and/or mouthpiece. Push your own mask up on to your forehead. He should now be on his back, your right hand supporting the back of his neck, his mouth and nose above water, neck stretched to clear the air flow. Open his mouth and ensure his tongue or any other obstruction is not interfering with the flow of air. Give EAR immediately. Breathing may have already stopped but the heart may still be beating so an attempt must be made to reintroduce breathing until someone who is medically qualified to make such a decision tells you to stop, or until a natural breathing rhythm is re-established.

Give *four good breaths* before commencing towing. Using the above towing hold you will find it possible to use your left arm as leverage on his left shoulder to roll the casualty's body slightly towards you, assisted by your right hand pushing up on the back of his neck. This will enable you to ensure a good seal over his nose without turning his head and possibly impeding the flow of air. As you roll him towards you use a stronger finning action to rise above him. Having given four good breaths before commencing towing, continue to give three or four breaths every five or six fin strokes.

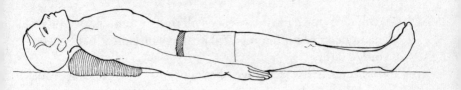

Fig 12 Position for EAR on land

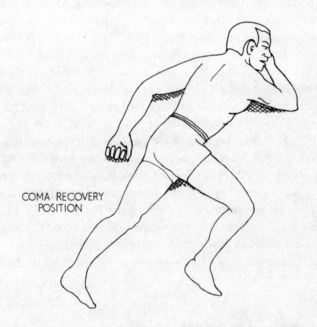

COMA RECOVERY
POSITION

Fig 13 Coma recovery position

Vital points to remember
1 Clear the mouth of any obstruction
2 Give four good breaths before commencing towing.
3 Keep the head tilted back and the neck extended at all times
  to ensure a clear passage of air.
4 Make sure a good seal over nose or mouth is achieved during
  EAR.
5 Continue EAR until a natural breathing rhythm is recovered
  by the subject.

61

6 The coastguard must have been alerted by another person so that a doctor or other medical help can be called to the scene immediately.

7 If the casualty is a diver he may also be suffering from embolism and/or decompression sickness.

He must be taken from the water and EAR continued if necessary. At this stage he should be lying on his back, arms by his sides and head tilted back (see Fig 12). Once breathing restarts the mouth should be checked regularly to ensure his tongue is not obstructing or that he has vomited in his throat or regurgitated sea water. In the case of the two latter events, roll the patient on to his side and clear his mouth with your fingers.

As the subject recovers he should be placed in the coma recovery position (see Fig 13), especially if still unconscious as he may 'swallow his tongue' or vomit. Keep him covered with warm clothing. It is vital that all casualties be seen by a medical practitioner even if apparently fully recovered. There may be a risk of pneumonia or congestion of the lungs.

The tow described above is a reliable and easily adapted method which can be used on swimmers and fully-kitted divers alike. There are other methods of course and two of these are mentioned below.

Fig 14 Non-contact tow

Non-contact tow

A non-contact tow involves the use of a towing aid and is suitable only for a conscious subject. If the subject is calm and co-operative then it will not endanger the rescuer to simply tow him by means of holding his assisted buoyancy life-jacket straps, finning on his back as shown in Fig 14.

Should the subject be likely to endanger the life of the rescuer then some other means must be used – anything which floats sufficiently to give him support such as a rescue belt or marker buoy. The rescuer is then able to tow him by holding on to the aid. Should the subject use the aid to try and reach the rescuer then the rescuer should release his hold on the aid thereby teaching the subject to stay at his own end of the aid.

Extended chin tow

Suitable to be used in a case where the subject is not breathing normally because it enables the rescuer to adopt the resuscitation position without difficulty. It also keeps the airway of the subject clear during towing and resuscitation. It requires the use of one hand only cupping the chin, leaving the other arm free. The rescuer may fin either on his back or on his side. It is only for use on a passive subject.

Practising in a pool

First find a victim. Commence rescue at the deep end with four quick breaths blown over the side of his face. Tilt the head at the correct angle for this. Still keeping the right towing hold fin down the pool giving EAR until you reach the shallow end. Turn him over at the same time placing his hands one on top of the other on the edge of the pool. Secure them by one of your own hands as you get out of the water. Standing, cross your arms holding both his hands. Use the slight buoyancy of the water to assist you in pulling him out of the water. Rest him with his waist on the edge of the pool. Gently but firmly move his legs on to the side of the pool so that he is face downwards.

Kneel by his side, turning his head away from you. Place the arm nearest you above his head. Take his far shoulder with one hand and his hip with the other. Hold his arm in place against his hip with your wrist. Roll him over to rest against your thighs, check his mouth for obstructions during these movements of the subject. Lower him on to his back. Check his mouth once more. Tilt his head back and continue EAR. Once he is breathing place him in the coma position (see Fig 13).

Deep rescue

The rescue of an unconscious diver from deep water by one diver is a hazardous operation and should not even be practised under controlled conditions unless the divers in question are both very fit and very experienced in deep diving and various aspects of emergency ascents and life-saving. However, it is possible to carry out providing one or, preferably, both divers are wearing assisted buoyancy life-jackets as is the common practice these days.

If the subject is struggling approach from behind and use a restraint hold. Release his weightbelt. Maintain a firm grip on the subject even if he is passive. If possible retain his mouthpiece and mask in position. If buoyancy is not achieved inflate his life-jacket. If insufficient buoyancy is still obtained then you will have to inflate your own life-jacket. Commence finning upwards. Ensure the subject is exhaling by pressing his diaphragm region as you ascend to make him exhale. Do not forget to watch your rate of ascent; if it is too fast, then vent some air from your own life-jacket and/or stop finning. Watch out for obstructions at the surface. At the surface inflate the subject's life-jacket by mouth and apply EAR as necessary. Summon help.

Remember
1 Do not ditch your own weightbelt. Should you lose hold of the subject you would be unable to get back down to him.

2 Try and make him exhale on ascent.
3 Watch the rate of ascent.

First aid

The possibility of injury is obviously increased when dealing with divers and boats. Some knowledge of simple first aid is a good idea for all divers but injuries must be dealt with only within the scope of the experience of the helpers. No drugs of any kind should be administered unless the person is qualified to do so. In serious cases more harm than good can be done if you have no training at all. However, every attempt must be made to remove the subject from the source of danger, make him comfortable and warm, reduce the flow of any bleeding.

Much depends on the circumstances in which you find yourself at the time. A course with a first aid association would arm you to cope with a variety of problems. First aid is really not something you can learn from a book but depending on the type of boat you have, the trip you are making, etc, a first aid kit of some kind should always be available in a watertight container on the boat. A kit could be based on the following items: first aid instructions; 3 or 4 large standard dressings; 2 triangular bandages; 4 safety pins; assorted sterile adhesive dressings; sterile cotton wool; and a rescue blanket or survival bag (a large polythene bag or sheeting taped up to form a bag the size of a sleeping bag will retain sufficient body heat to be used as a survival bag and gives protection from wind and rain).

Remember
If faced with a serious condition, eg cardiac arrest, hypothermia, bends, broken bones, etc, an attempt must be made to get the earliest possible medical assistance for the subject, while attempts are made to keep him alive and/or improve his situation or at least prevent his condition from worsening.

7
Aqualung Equipment

Regulators

There are basically two types – the single hose and the twin hose regulator. Both of these are now manufactured with two stages. There are other types available probably secondhand namely, single stage single and twin hose regulators, also single hose upstream action regulators. Depending on the country in which you learn and carry out your diving you will use the single or twin hose two-stage regulator. In Britain the most commonly used regulator is the single hose two-stage downstream action type but the twin hose is more popular in some parts of the world.

Function of single hose two-stage downstream regulator
A cylinder is filled with air to a working pressure between 2,250–3,250psi dependent on the cylinder. It would not be possible to breathe air at such a pressure. The first stage of the regulator is designed to reduce this to between 140–190psi which depends on the make of regulator.

The first stage is attached to the pillar valve of the cylinder, the second stage is next to the mouthpiece. The two stages are connected by a low-pressure flexible hose about one centimetre in diameter (see Fig 15). Air travels through the hose to the second stage and mouthpiece and thence to the lungs. The exhaled air flows directly into the water through the exhaust valve in the second stage. The first stage is worked either on a piston or diaphragm system.

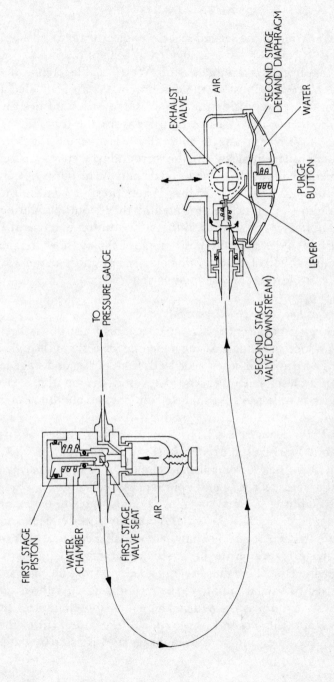

Fig 15 Single hose two-stage downstream regulator

The function of the second stage is to give air to the diver on demand. It is in two sections divided by a diaphragm. In front of the diaphragm is a purge button. Water is able to enter the front chamber and rest on the diaphragm. As air is inhaled a vacuum is created inside the second stage which pushes the diaphragm inwards. This in turn activates the lever in the second stage valve. Air is thus allowed to enter the rear chamber until it equalises with the surrounding water pressure. This method allows the diver air on demand. The purge button will provide a free flow of air. When pressed against the diaphragm the levers are activated as they would be during inspiration. Air will flow until the purge button is released.

If using single hose the positioning of the cylinder, or the swimming action of the diver do not have any effect on the way air is fed to him by his demand valve.

Function of twin hose two-stage regulator

In this regulator the entire demand mechanism and both stages are contained in a single casing which fits directly to the pillar valve. There are two hoses. One leads from the second stage to the mouthpiece. The other leads back from the mouthpiece to the water chamber. Air is exhausted into the surrounding water through holes in the casing (see Fig 16).

Air flows from the pillar valve into both stages of the regulator. The first stage reduces pressure to about 110psi. The second stage has an equalising chamber which is separated from the water by a rubber diaphragm. Air collects on one side of this diaphragm. Small openings permit water to enter the front chamber on the other side. As the diver descends the air pressure in the equalising chambers remains equal to that of the water pressure on the other side of the diaphragm.

The 'dry' side of the diaphragm has a lever valve mechanism connected to the air supply of the second stage. As the diver inhales a vacuum is created in the equalising chamber. Air flows from the second stage down the hose, into the mouthpiece, to the lungs. The diaphragm is depressed by water

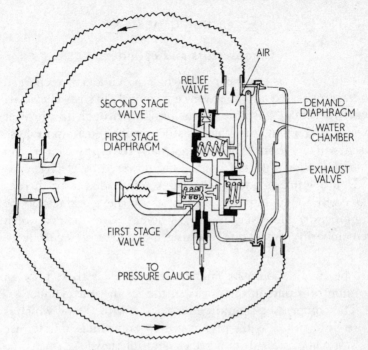

Fig 16 Twin hose two-stage regulator

pressure on the wet side and it thus opens the valve leading to the first stage air supply. The first stage opens and air flows through the second stage on the dry side of the diaphragm, forcing it back into a neutral position as air and surrounding water pressure equalise. The air flow from the first stage ceases until the next inspiration. Expired air travels to the water chamber along the exhaust hose and escapes through holes in the casing into the surrounding water.

If using a twin hose regulator the cylinder should be worn so that the regulator is level with the shoulder blades. In normal face-down finning this ensures the regulator is almost at the same pressure as the lungs of the diver. Should the diver swim on his back, air will be delivered more readily but not uncontrollably. The alteration in air flow takes place due to the fact that the regulator would then be at a lower pressure than that exerted on the diver's lungs.

AQUALUNG EQUIPMENT

Compressors and cylinders

A compressor is the means by which a cylinder is recharged with compressed air. They vary enormously in size. They start with the small portable petrol design, through the heavier diesel-run compressor which is still portable, just, up to those used in diving shops. These are normally the type which are run in conjunction with 'air banks' and powered by electricity.

In a beginner's book such as this is intended to be there is no room to go into the intricacies of the workings of the compressor. However, there are some major points worth remembering by anyone who uses a compressor regularly.

1 The filters should be changed regularly as these play an important part in the purity of the air in your cylinder.
2 The compressor should be lubricated with the oil which is recommended by the manufacturer. Some oil is unfit for use in a compressor from a safety point of view.
3 The compressor should be 'bled' at the drain taps in accordance with instructions, during filling of cylinders. This reduces the possibility of a wet fill and subsequent damage to the interior of the cylinders over the long term.
4 When operating the compressor the air intake hose should always be upwind of the engine exhaust so that the intake is not contaminated by noxious fumes (see carbon monoxide poisoning on p 40). A compressor should never be operated where there is a danger of the air being contaminated, eg a busy seaside car park.
5 Even the best portable compressors are fairly noisy so do not operate one where it can cause annoyance to others.

Pillar valves
The pillar valve permits air to be held in the cylinder under high pressure. It is also the means by which air is allowed to escape into the regulator. There are several types on the market but most of these today are of the balanced variety (see Fig 17) and

70

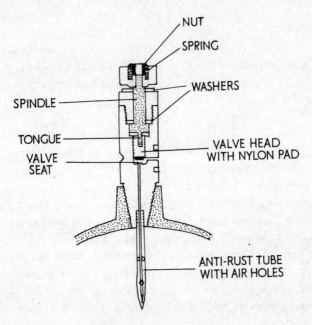

NUT

SPRING

WASHERS

SPINDLE

TONGUE

VALVE SEAT

VALVE HEAD WITH NYLON PAD

ANTI-RUST TUBE WITH AIR HOLES

Fig 17 Balanced pillar valve

either crossflow or upright. At one time aluminium pillar valves were fitted but were found to suffer from electrolysis around the 0–ring groove. Although previously it was thought that a combination of brass pillar valve in aluminium cylinder would also produce this effect, this was found to be untrue and a large number of cylinders are now fitted with a brass pillar valve.

Even a cylinder which is regularly inspected can have flakes of rust forming inside, therefore a small tube extends from the bottom of all pillar valves down below the level of the shoulders of the cylinder. Thus the particles are prevented from entering the valve and possibly interfering with the air supply. There are different means of sealing when a pillar valve is put into a cylinder, these depend on whether the thread is tapering or parallel. Never attempt to remove or replace a pillar valve yourself, in doing so the threads may be damaged.

A balanced valve should not be stiff to turn on. A collection of salt, or some other problem may be the cause. Silicone spray can help but the reasons should be investigated. An occasional use of silicone grease can help protect the valve. Always wash the valve off with fresh water after use. Salt has a corrosive effect and, when dry, can accumulate on the spindle.

Reserve valves
A pressure gauge is used to measure the contents of a cylinder so that the diver knows how quickly he is using his air.

An alternative in common use is the reserve valve (see Fig 18). This valve is fitted to the cylinder and has to be set in the dive position before going underwater. As the pressure in the cylinder drops to a low level, approximately 30atm, the mechanism in the valve restricts the flow of air to the demand valve. At this warning the diver operates a rod on the side of the cylinder which activates the reserve. The spring-loaded valve is withdrawn from its seating and allows free flow of reserve air to the regulator.

The important point to remember with reserve valves is that

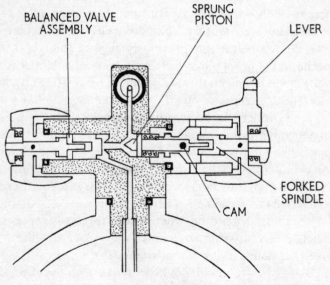

Fig 18 Reserve valve

they must be reset before each dive. If the valve is not reset then the restriction of air when it comes will be because the cylinder is almost empty, not as a warning to switch to reserve. Some divers do remove the rods from the valves to avoid the possibility of the valve being operated accidentally without their knowledge by being caught in kelp or similar. If the rod is removed then the valve has to be operated by hand.

Pressure gauge

This gauge is attached to the first stage of the regulator by means of a flexible hose and is commonly referred to as the contents gauge. Air travels from the pillar valve through the first stage into the hose and the gauge indicates the pressure of the cylinder contents. You can assess from the pressure reading whether the cylinder is full, half-full, etc. The general practice is to surface when the reading has dropped to not less than 30atm if no decompression stops have to be carried out.

Cylinders

There are regulations governing the use of high pressure cylinders in all countries but these vary. Generally speaking however, cylinders carry markings to show the following information:

1 Date of manufacture and test.
2 Marks and dates of any subsequent tests (cylinders have to be tested regularly).
3 Manufacturer's marks.
4 Specification (steel or aluminium, thickness of cylinder walls in relation to working pressure, etc).
5 Working pressure and test pressure.

Cylinders are manufactured in galvanised steel or aluminium. Aluminium is popular because it is rust-free and therefore should have a longer life. It is also lighter. They are manufactured in several sizes and some working pressures vary up to 200 bars (200atm). When choosing the size of cylinder for your own use your lung requirements are obviously the most important factor. Do you use your air quickly? If so, you will require a cylinder with a larger capacity. What type of diving do you intend to do? Do you intend to go in for deep diving as much as possible? Again you have to bear in mind the heavier air consumption under greater pressure, plus air for decompression stops. As a novice you may find it takes a while for your breathing rhythm to become natural and you will use air more quickly than a more experienced diver. However, as a novice, it is unlikely that you will be attempting much in the way of decompression diving.

Aluminium bottles are lighter if you are going to have to carry your equipment some distance. Some cylinders are longer than others so bear in mind your height and the length of your back. If you have long trips on an inflatable and have to wear your cylinder during them a too-long cylinder can be uncomfortable. Some divers start with a small lightweight cylinder which is ideal for pool training and shallow diving. Later as they progress they buy a second larger cylinder, or another cylinder the same size which can be twinned with the original, using a manifold, therefore making up a twinset for use when the occasion of a deep dive arises.

Twinsets can be unwieldy and, for the most part, unnecessary unless you are exceptionally heavy on air or intend to make deep diving, over thirty metres, your life's work. It should be stated that there are some purpose-built neat, relatively lightweight twinsets on the market if you want to make the investment.

As usual, it comes back to what you want to spend at this stage. You can save money when buying cylinders by looking for a good secondhand one. A cylinder must be in test before it can be sold through a diving shop. Make sure, whoever you buy from, that it is a new test certificate or, if almost out of test, insist on a test being carried out before purchasing. A cylinder in Great Britain must be tested three years from the date of manufacture and every two years thereafter. Normally shops will not fill an out-of-test cylinder. Make sure the pillar valve has not been damaged and does not leak (it could be just the O-ring but check just the same). Some makes of cylinder can present problems as the pillar valve does not allow the regulator to seat properly and a complete seal is not achieved either when filling or when fitting the regulator. Make sure your equipment is compatible. When buying gear for the first time ask an experienced diver to examine it with you, especially if buying secondhand.

8
Additional
Diving Equipment

There are numerous items of equipment, in addition to the cylinders and regulators; some are vital to safe diving, others are useful but not essential. One essential if diving in colder waters is a wetsuit, or possibly a drysuit.

Wetsuits

There are several types of diving suits available but only those in most common use are being dealt with here. Most sport divers use the nylon-lined unicellular foam rubber suits known as neoprene suits. Tiny air bubbles incorporated into the material provide the insulation by allowing water to seep into the suit next to the body. This thin film of water is quickly warmed by the body heat. Underclothing is not necessary with this type of suit. The effectiveness of the suit depends upon the quality of material and the fit. A good suit fits like a second skin over the body leaving no openings or pockets for cold water to enter or collect beneath the suit.

Suits can be bought off-the-peg or made-to-measure although the latter cost slightly more. Also available are kits from which you can make up your own suit. Suits are also made up in a variety of different finishes, some smooth, some textured. Generally, they are sold as a four piece suit; jacket, trousers, hood and boots. Many divers start off with a suit 5mm thick as being a good basic suit in the medium price range.

Later, as they dive deeper and for longer periods they change for the thicker neoprene, eg 6.5mm or for double-lined suits which are hardwearing and warm.

Long-johns covering from ankle to shoulder (sleeveless) instead of trousers give a second layer over the trunk of the body and make a lot of difference to comfort. A jacket with hood attached or a hood with an extra large yoke to tuck in both help to prevent cold water seeping in down the back of the jacket collar. A cold spine quickly makes the rest of the body feel cold and cuts short the dive. A jacket to pull over the head and having no zip is good from the warmth point of view. One-piece suits with hood attached and front zip are comfortable. Vests of varying thicknesses of neoprene can be purchased to wear under the jacket if you find you are cold in your first suit. It does save the expense of purchasing a long-john but is not really as comfortable or as efficient.

Boots provided with a suit are usually soft sole (all neoprene). If you know you are going to do a lot of tramping up and down stony beaches then hard sole boots will last longer, they are also kinder to the feet on land. These are ordinary neoprene boots but have a rubber sole. Make sure you get a good make as one or two makes have a history of soles which start coming off quite soon after purchase and are never the same again. Alternatively, plastic Saracen sandals or galoshes can be worn on land to protect a soft sole boot. If purchasing hard sole boots you may find you need bigger fins, depending on the type of fins you use.

Gloves or mitts are sold separately and are well worth the investment. They provide the necessary protection from sharp rocks, wrecks, etc, and help reduce the loss in body heat.

Drysuits

The neoprene drysuit is used by numerous professional divers, particularly those who have to be able to swim and manoeuvre easily underwater. It is constructed of double nylon-lined foam neoprene. A zip starts at the base of the neck, runs down the back, under the crutch, and up the front. This makes the suit very easy to put on and to remove. The suit is made in one piece with hood and rubber boots attached. There are rubber seals at neck and cuffs and a finer rubber seal around the face.

The suit is inflatable by direct feed from the cylinder. Two valves on the chest allow the suit to be either inflated or deflated at a touch. The only problems likely to be encountered are those similar to those connected with the use of the ABLJ underwater although this type of suit is best not purchased by an inexperienced diver. Apart from the safety aspect, the thickness and buoyancy of the suit mean some alteration in finning action.

Ideally an undersuit of the thick 'woolly bear' type is worn underneath. As long as the suit is properly cared for and works efficiently the diver should remain dry.

There are several makes of one-piece neoprene drysuit on the market; often without the integral hood but with neoprene boots attached. Most often they are zipped across the shoulders. All of them cost rather more than a conventional wetsuit. The diver has to be sure that the type of diving he does warrants the expenditure.

The rubber drysuit was mainly used by professional divers, particularly those doing maintenance work where quick movements and long distance swimming was not required. Made of rubber, the chief disadvantage was that it would, if not properly cared for, perish and therefore leak under pressure. A special powder or talcum powder used liberally on the suit helped prevent perishing. The suit was usually inflated via a small bottle worn on a belt around the waist. To deflate it one arm was held above the head and the cuff opened slightly allowing air to escape. Help was needed to stretch the opening sufficiently to enter the suit through the neck. The neck seal was completed by a metal collar which was screwed in place.

These suits are now manufactured from rubber-coated tricot and do not rot. They are easy to clean and repair. The styles vary from heavy-duty work suits to specially-designed sport diving suits. The conventional-style neck-entry suit can now be donned without assistance; alternatively entry can be through a shoulder zip opening or a vertical zip from the top of the integral hood down to the waist. Suits are designed with or without integral hood. Inflation is by direct feed from the cylinder and deflation by the outlet valve on shoulder or hood. The basic 'Navy Drybag' style without valves is still produced. The suits are suitable for diving in warm or ice-cold water as the insulation can be varied to suit personal requirements. Specially designed polyesterfoam undersuits are on the market.

Prices of both types of drysuit are beginning to come down and thus they are increasing in popularity with sport divers, particularly those who become involved in long-term underwater projects.

Other equipment

An aqualung diver kitted up is shown in Fig 19. The equipment illustrated is now dealt with individually.

Weightbelts
The buoyancy caused by air trapped in a wetsuit must be offset by wearing a belt carrying lead weights. These belts are available in rubber, or in nylon webbings. Avoid the type which gives too much underwater as you will always be adjusting your weightbelt. All belts must have a quick release buckle which can be opened quickly and easily with one hand in an emergency calling for such an action as ditching your weightbelt. Weighted correctly a diver will be able to swim comfortably underwater without effort.

Mask, fins and snorkel
These items have already been dealt with in Chapter 5.

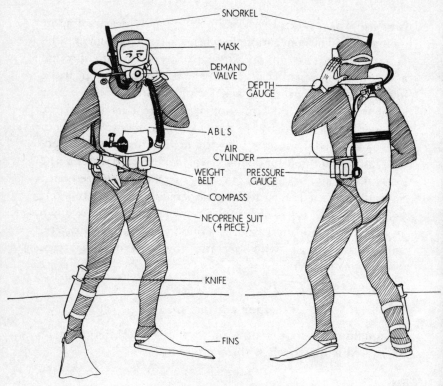

SNORKEL

MASK

DEMAND
VALVE

DEPTH
GAUGE

ABLS

AIR
CYLINDER

WEIGHT
BELT

PRESSURE
GAUGE

COMPASS

NEOPRENE SUIT
(4 PIECE)

KNIFE

FINS

Fig 19 Aqualung diver kitted up

Adjustable buoyancy life-jacket (ABLJ)
These are dealt with in Chapter 10. The reason for this is that
there are certain risks in using them underwater so that it is
safest to discuss their function and training at the same time.

Diving knife
A knife should be worn by snorkellers and aqualung divers
alike. The real purpose of the knife is for use on entangling net
or line underwater. Some knives look elegant but would be no
good for any sort of heavy use. The knife must be sturdy, made
of stainless steel with a cutting edge on one side, a saw edge on
the other. Preferably the haft of the knife should go through the

80

actual solid rubber handle where a screw will hold it firmly in place. Buy a knife which you know you can easily grasp with a clumsy gloved hand. Wear the knife in the sheath at all times when not in use, never carry it around in your hand. The sheath will strap to thigh or calf. Some will attach to the weightbelt – not really a good idea as if you have to ditch the weightbelt you will lose a knife as well. Some can be worn on a separate belt around the waist but this does mean yet more encumbrance added to weightbelt, cylinder harness, and ABLJ straps.

Depth gauge
An essential, not a trimming. From the start wear a depth gauge and get used to checking the reading. When deep water diving it will be necessary to be accurate in checking depth and time for decompression stops.

Basically there are two types, the capillary and the bourdon tube. The capillary relies on water entering with increased depth and pressure and the gauge reacts directly to this. This type is really best used only in shallow water diving. The bourdon tube is oil-filled and sealed against entry of sand. The water pressure on the case acts on the oil which in turn sets the bourdon tube to move the gauge needle. Some gauges are not sealed and water pressure acts through a simple mesh filter.

Diver's compass
This enables a diver to navigate a straight line underwater, allowing for two things: one being the pull of the tide, the other being that one leg may be stronger than the other in finning and may tend to send you slightly off course. Being underwater has a disorientating effect and you can lose your way immediately you reach the seabed. Experienced divers can find their way around by 'landmarks', tidal patterns on the seabed, etc, but this does depend on reasonable visibility so a compass is a necessity.

The simple clear type of luminous compass is best for diving. A moveable bezel by which you can set your bearing makes life much easier. Do not buy something you cannot readily understand; your mind does not always function with the same clarity underwater as it does at the surface.

Watches

These are an expensive item but essential, especially if decompression diving. A watch should be waterproof, luminous and be able to withstand a minimum 50m depth pressure. The face should be easily read in murky water. The bezel should, ideally, move only one way so that there is less likelihood of it being moved accidentally underwater after setting. The strap should be strong thick rubber or strong plastic (plastic can split eventually but is reasonably long lasting). Some divers prefer the stainless steel bands which look better if the watch is also worn on land, as most are. However, one watch at least has been lost when the catch snagged on a piece of equipment, gave way, and disappeared overboard. Underwater it is safest to wear any watch so that the wrist of your neoprene glove can be pulled over it as added protection against loss or damage.

Harnesses

The types of harness and back packs available for use with the cylinder are numerous. It is really a question of what is comfortable for you. It should be strong, the clips which hold the cylinder in place should work efficiently and the harness must have a quick release buckle on the waist strap.

Diver buoys

Marker buoys are in general use amongst divers. Divers have increased vastly in numbers in recent years and so have other water users. A buoy is essential for your boat cover to be able to keep track of you and for other boats to give you a wide berth. It is very difficult to keep track of just the diver's bubbles. It only takes a few seconds of inattention – trouble with the engine for example – and you and the boat can be some distance apart.

This is particularly true if the state of the tide has been wrongly assessed or there is a sudden change in the direction of the wind. The buoy provides a means of communication from surface to diver by means of pre-arranged rope signals, eg if the weather suddenly turns very bad the boat cover can tell you to come up.

Mooring buoys in fluorescent orange or white connected by strong fine line to a reel held by the diver are commonly used. A good marker available is in blue and white with a diving flag on top. No mistakes can be made by people on the surface if you are using one of this type. At first buoys can be a nuisance but you will find with practice, that you rarely snag on rocks. When surfacing, keep the line taut as you reel it in. This way you avoid knots and entanglements. More important you surface directly alongside the buoy which is the safest place to be.

Some clubs use buddy lines, particularly when training novices. These are lines, a few metres long, which are attached to novice and dive leader or instructor. More often, the instructor will carry the reel of a buoy line and the novice holds on to the line a short distance away and parallel to the instructor. Alternatively, he may reverse the position, giving the reel to the novice to carry. That way, in the unlikely event of becoming separated the instructor can surface and trace his novice by finding the buoy and following the line down. The aim of buddy diving is to stay together at all times in case of an emergency but occasional separations do happen. As a novice you should not risk going off on your own, stay glued to your instructor at all times.

Diver's flag

A diver's flag must be flown by a boat while divers are actually in the water. It indicates to other users of the sea that divers are underwater and they should exercise caution in the area. The flag is divided vertically into two colours, blue and white.

ADDITIONAL DIVING EQUIPMENT

Fluorescent hoods
A number of divers wear fluorescent orange hoods over their black neoprene hoods. These do show up well at sea and help the boat cover, and other boats, to spot them in the water. They can be purchased ready-made or are easy to make yourself from a kit.

Torch
Essential for diving at night and can be useful when diving in dark or deep water. Must be waterproof (ordinary torches will work in an emergency but quickly corrode on the surface after a dive). During night diving the beam from a torch reveals brilliantly the true colours of the marine life.

Various accessories
1 *Fin grips.* These are Y-shaped rubber straps which can be slipped over the fin and ankle to keep fins in place. They can be made out of old inner tube, scraps of neoprene, or purchased.
2 *'Goody' bag.* This is any bag used for carrying the catch, eg fish, crab, lobster and it can be purchased purpose-made. Otherwise, a strong nylon mesh shopping bag, open weave and rot-proof and allowing water to escape will do.
3 *Handspear.* A handspear must have a point at one end and a hook at the other. They can be purchased but are easily made. Care should be exercised when putting them aboard inflatable boats. Keep a cork on the pointed end when aboard.
Remember when hunting for supper stay well away from pots, nets or lines.

Decompression meter
These meters should not be used by amateur divers. They are used by some professional divers but with caution and within the limits marked. The meters are useful for divers who have to carry out several dives of differing depths and duration in one day. It acts on a totting-up scale which gradually creeps up to a danger line. Before that line is reached the diver should leave

the water and rest until the needle has dropped back sufficiently for him to go into the water again.

Care of equipment

Sea water, pool chemicals and strong sunlight are very bad for diving equipment. Diving equipment is expensive. To ensure a long and safe life it helps to follow a few simple rules. They sound, and are, a nuisance after returning tired from a long day of diving. If you can get organised on a regular basis it makes it less painful.

1 Always wash *all* your gear in fresh water after a diving trip. A tub in the garden and an outside tap are ideal. The bath is just as good but may be unpopular with the rest of the household.
2 Pay particular attention to pillar valve and 0-ring, demand valve, crown and bezel of watch, life-jacket fittings and depth gauge. Sand or grit under the bezel of the watch or in the pillar valve can cause expensive damage in time. Large pieces of grit in the demand valve could interfere with the efficient working of it.
3 Hang your suit to dry outside, preferably not in blazing sun. Dry off the other equipment with a towel.

Long-term reminders
1 Make sure your cylinder and life-jacket bottle are checked and tested regularly.
2 Never store your cylinder empty for long periods. Store full or half-full.
3 Regular servicing of your demand valve will ensure it is safe to use.
4 Leave some air in the life-jacket when not in use. Do not roll it up and put it back in your bag under all the other equipment.
5 Check gear occasionally for splits, tears or cracks.

9
Aqualung Training in the Pool and Signals

All training with an aqualung should be carried out under supervision.

Technique for kitting up

You are standing at the edge of the pool surrounded by all the necessary equipment. The first step is to fit the demand valve on the cylinder.

1 Check that the 0–ring in the pillar valve is in good condition and seated properly in its groove. This is to ensure a proper seal.
2 Clear the pillar valve of any dust or moisture by letting out a small burst of air.
3 Put the clamp of the regulator over the top of the pillar valve, making sure it is properly seated. Tighten the screw. Do not overtighten, a firm grip is all that is required, the pressure of the air passing from valve to first stage will complete the seal.
4 Turn on the air gradually to full, then turn the tap back half or one turn. While turning on the air make sure the face of the pressure gauge is turned away from you. Once turned on check the pressure of the cylinder contents on the gauge.
5 Take a few breaths through the mouthpiece. This checks that the demand valve is functioning. At the same time watch the needle on the pressure gauge. It should not move, if it does

this may indicate that the air is not turned on properly or that there may be a malfunction.

6 Turn off the pillar valve. If the needle on the gauge falls there could be a leakage somewhere in a connection.

7 Make sure you turn the air back on.

8 After use you will want to remove the regulator from the cylinder. First turn off air at the pillar valve fully. Next press the purge valve on the mouthpiece so that air escapes. Press until the needle on the pressure gauge has fallen back to zero. You will then be able to unscrew and remove the regulator. Allow a burst of air into the opening on the first stage to dry out any moisture. Replace dustcap.

9 When not in use keep cylinders lying down and out of the way of other pool users.

Remember from the start, always check your gear yourself. Never rely on someone else to turn on your air for you.

For pool training without a suit, you will find a T-shirt or similar will stop the harness buckles from chafing ; it will also keep you warm longer.

Lift up the cylinder sliding one arm through a shoulder strap, then ease on the other. Lean forward slightly as you tighten the straps so that the weight of the bottle is taken along your back. Make sure that it is not too high in the harness or you will hit your head on the pillar valve underwater. Tuck the contents gauge under your arm and through the strap of the harness. That way you will be able to reach it easily for checking. Fasten the waist strap so that it is comfortable.

When you are fully kitted up, including mask, fins and snorkel, enter the shallow end. Sit on the bottom of the pool for a few minutes until you are breathing in a relaxed manner. When you have become accustomed to the equipment, swim around the pool for a short time. *Breathe normally at all times — never hold your breath on ascent.*

Next, carry out a buoyancy check. Lie on the bottom of the pool and breathe in. See how far you rise. If you are wearing a neoprene jacket or suit for warmth you will need some form of weightbelt. Experiment with weights until you can lie on the bottom of the pool, face down, breathing normally. If you take a deep breath you should rise slightly off the bottom, when you breathe out hard you should sink again. This means you have your buoyancy at the right level. Swim around getting used to the deep end of the pool.

There are a series of exercises which should be carried out until they can be performed with confidence. These are not a waste of time. They are vital to give the diver the knowledge to cope with the disorientating effect that being underwater can sometimes have. Also certain problems may arise and the diver should be able to handle these calmly.

Mask clearing
If you are careless putting on your mask it could flood underwater. It may come loose or get knocked. Knowing how to clear it in such an event makes a diver more confident.

During snorkel training you have already practised swimming without a mask but it is a good idea to do so wearing an aqualung and swimming underwater. The easiest way is to follow the side of the pool or a line along the bottom, one hand keeping in contact with the tiles. You must get used to swimming with your eyes open underwater. Now, wearing the mask, kneel on the bottom of the pool with the water covering your head. If you have difficulty in staying on the bottom wear a weightbelt. Breathing normally, remove your mask. To help break the air seal blow into it down your nose as you lift it away from your face, from the bottom of the mask. Holding the mask out in front of you place the strap neatly over the front of the mask, inside out. Next, make sure your hair is all out of the way. Place the mask against your face. Put the strap over the back of your head. You are wearing a mask at least half full of water. Tilting your head back, look towards the surface. Exhale through your nose. At the same time pull the lower edge of the mask gently away from your face. Just enough to break the seal.

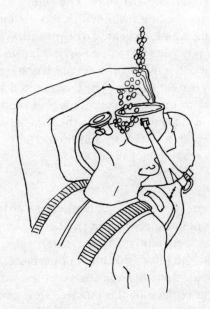

Fig 20 Putting on and clearing a face mask underwater

The exhaled air will force the water out under the bottom of the mask. Do not pull the mask too far out as you will simply keep flooding it and no amount of blowing will clear it. This method is shown in Fig 20. Alternatively, lie on your side and hold the upper side of the mask against your face while blowing water out via the lower side.

Purge valves are fitted to some masks and these are easy to use. Merely holding the top of the mask against the face and exhaling through the nose will flush the water out via the purge valve. Even though these are available it is important that you practise the mask-clearing procedure until you can do it automatically. When you have mastered it you should move to deeper water and continue practising for a while.

Forward and backward rolls
Now you are becoming more confident it is a good time to practise backward and forward rolls. You will have already perfected these in snorkelling training but it is obviously a bit different wearing full aqualung gear. To begin with you will feel ungainly. Very quickly you will realise that it is far easier as you can use your breath either to help you descend or to keep you off the bottom halfway through a turn. The best method is to take a breath as you start to go into a roll. This will increase your buoyancy and you will avoid landing on the tiles on your back. Take care to take enough breath to slightly increase buoyancy but not enough to make you ascend.

Mouthpiece removal
Kneel on the bottom of the pool submerged in fairly shallow water. Remove the mouthpiece holding it at arm's length out to your side. Breathe out gently. At the same time hold the mouthpiece so that the purge button is uppermost. Press the button to start the air flowing and thus expel the water. With the air still flowing replace in the mouth. Blow out to clear remaining water, if any. Breathe as normal. Move to the deep end and continue until relaxed. If you are borrowing

equipment for your pool training you will not always have the same valve. Make a point of remembering on which side your demand valve hangs. Generally it is over the right shoulder but some are left handed.

Procedure with twin hose regulators

It is a good idea to familiarise yourself with both procedures even if you do not intend wearing a twin hose regulator yourself. You may find yourself with a buddy who wears one.

Assembling the equipment is much the same as with a single hose. The important thing to remember is the positioning of the cylinder in the back pack. If it is too high the flow of air will be restricted; too low and air will be pushed at the diver. Having donned the cylinder, identify which hose is which. Hold one tube and squeeze firmly while blowing through the mouthpiece. If you can blow out then you are holding the intake hose; if you cannot, then it is the exhaust hose. Generally the intake hose (that through which air is supplied to the diver) is on the right-hand side.

Mask-clearing procedures can be carried out in the same way as with a single hose regulator.

Mouthpiece removal of twin hose regulator
Hold the mouthpiece at head height and air will flow freely. When lowered to chest level the flow stops. Once removed, hold the mouthpiece at head height so that the air is flowing, then tilt it towards your face and lower it into your mouth. Blow out to expel any remaining water via exhaust hose. In the unlikely event of your letting go of the hoses underwater they will float up over your head gushing air. An easy way to retrieve them is to execute a backward roll so that they appear above your face where you can reach them.

Flooding of twin hose regulator
A very rare occurence but the non-return valve just may fail and

the hoses flood. Should this happen roll on to your left side, or the side where the exhaust hose is lowest. Blow out hard. Continue to roll over on to your back. This should carry the water down the hose and out of the exhaust.

Methods of pool entry

You have practised in snorkelling equipment, now practise fully kitted-up before you have to enter the sea from the side of a boat. Make sure the water is clear before you enter, ie no obstructions.

Giant stride
Stand on the side of the pool, feet on the edge, fins overhanging. Place one hand over mask and mouthpiece (if you lose either going into the sea you could have problems). The other hand should be on your waist strap holding down your cylinder. If it is slightly loose it could come up and the pillar valve will hit the back of your head as you enter the water. Lean slightly forward. Take a large step out and down into the water, turning slightly as you do so.

Forward and backward rolls
This entry is the same as when wearing snorkelling equipment but hold on to mask, mouthpiece and waist strap as above. The most common way of entering the water from the side of a boat is to sit on the gunwales and roll in backwards.
Remember do not hold your breath, breathe normally at all times.

Doff and don of equipment

It is stressed that this should not be practised unless under supervision.

During your snorkel training you practised removing and retrieving mask, fins and snorkel. Now practise removing and replacing the aqualung. This will be carried out in the deep end. Remember to equalise the pressure on your ears as you descend. During the exercise relax as much as possible and do not take great gulps of air. This will increase your buoyancy and you will rise off the bottom of the pool. It makes very hard work of a relatively simple exercise.

Kneel on the bottom of the pool breathing normally. Undo the quick release buckle with one hand and slacken the shoulder straps. Remove the cylinder by reaching behind the head and grasping the top of the back pack with one hand. Pull it up over the head with one hand on the cylinder and one on the back pack. Place it so that it rests on the bottom of the pool with the back pack and the pillar valve facing towards you. Keep breathing from the mouthpiece. Arrange the straps so that they are free when you attempt to replace the cylinder on your back. Breathe for a few seconds and then replace the cylinder on your back.

To replace the cylinder put your arms through the straps so that your hands support it. Take the strain by bending your elbows out to keep the straps taut. Lift the cylinder up and bring it down behind the head sliding the straps down the arms and over the shoulders at the same time. Make sure the pillar valve is the right way up. Settle it on your back, tighten shoulder straps and fasten the waist buckle.

The next stage is to remove the cylinder and mouthpiece and weightbelt. If you are wearing a neoprene jacket or suit for warmth *do not* remove the weightbelt as you will rise quickly and will find it difficult, if not impossible, to get back down to your cylinder. Arrange straps neatly. Remove mouthpiece and place it so that it can easily be retrieved. Surface, *exhaling. Do not hold your breath on ascent.* Having surfaced, rest for a few seconds. Note the position of the cylinder then dive down to retrieve. On the bottom, replace mouthpiece, then cylinder, and weightbelt if it has been removed.

Finally, remove all equipment, including mask, fins and snorkel, and then surface. Before doing so, place your mask where you can pick it up immediately after you have replaced the mouthpiece in your mouth. Clear mask, don cylinder, fins and other equipment.

Persevere with these exercises until you can do them in a relaxed and confident manner. The key to coping is to breathe normally. Even if you feel a bit edgy on the first attempts to surface and retrieve, keep calm and go on with it. If you start to float off the bottom, breathe out steadily. Lie on the bottom and regain normal breathing rhythm. Concentrate hard on what you are doing and your breathing will come naturally. If you really must surface and try again, do so. Do not surface in a panic, breathe out on ascent.

Buddy breathing

This is an emergency procedure which must be mastered in the pool. If you or your buddy should be in the position where air is not coming through on demand then you may have to share from one mouthpiece to reach the surface. Just in case such an emergency should arise it is a good thing to have practised to the point where you feel fairly confident about being able to do so without endangering yourself or your buddy.

You and your partner should kneel on the bottom facing each other, both fully kitted up and having previously decided who is to be the donor. Each diver holds with one hand to a strap of the other so that they remain facing. The donor takes the mouthpiece from his mouth (having taken two good breaths) and passes it towards his partner, air flowing. His partner uses his free hand to help guide it to his mouth. He then takes two breaths and the procedure is reversed. They continue with the exercise each taking two breaths before relinquishing the mouthpiece, in between, breathing out. When they have established a relaxed rhythm they can start swimming around the pool to get used to sharing air while finning. During buddy breathing firm contact between divers must be maintained at all times.

Twin hose buddy breathing

If using a twin hose regulator for buddy breathing the receiver of the air should be at a slightly higher level than the donor. The mouthpiece should be presented to him with the air flowing to ensure that he receives air immediately. After taking his breaths he returns the mouthpiece in the same way. The divers have to remain facing at all times to enable the mouthpiece to pass freely from donor to buddy and back.

General

Each person needs to build his confidence at his own speed. Some take to the snorkel and aqualung naturally and have no trouble at all. Others find that there is one particular item which worries them, eg mask clearing or removing and replacing aqualung equipment underwater. You must go at your own pace. Do not get involved in a race with other trainees and force yourself on faster than you really wish to go. The aim is to be a good safe diver and to enjoy yourself, both in the pool as well as in the sea. Even when experienced, most divers find it useful to practise all these procedures in the pool periodically. This is particularly true if they have had a lay-off for a while as the exercises help rebuild fitness and stamina as well as improving breath control.

Remember

1 Breathe normally at all times, *never hold your breath on ascent.*

2 If you feel pressure on your ears on descent equalise the pressure, do not wait for pain.

3 Relax and breathe regularly during exercises, deep breaths will cause you to rise off the bottom, away from your equipment.

4 Always take responsibility for checking your own equipment.

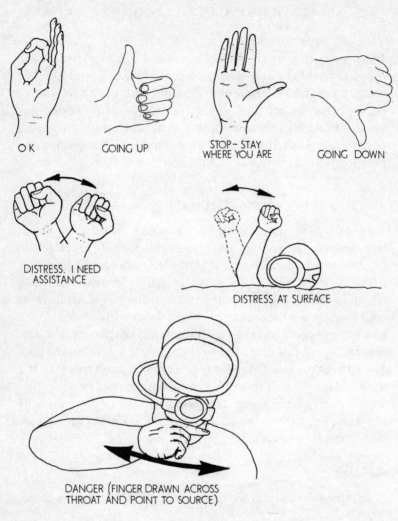

O K

GOING UP

STOP – STAY
WHERE YOU ARE

GOING DOWN

DISTRESS. I NEED
ASSISTANCE

DISTRESS AT SURFACE

DANGER (FINGER DRAWN ACROSS
THROAT AND POINT TO SOURCE)

Fig 21 Signals

Signals

One of the attractions of being underwater is the lack of noise. No one can talk to you or at you. However, you have to communicate somehow with your buddy and there are a few basic signals which are used all the time (see Fig 21).

OK. All is well
The finger and thumb of the right (or left) hand combine to form a circle. Other fingers remain upright. This is used between divers to communicate that all is well on the surface or underwater. Also used to acknowledge or agree to a signal such as change of direction, etc.

Ascend and descend
Clenched fist, thumb extended, pointed down or towards the surface. Used to signal descent or ascent. Usually followed by the OK signal and replied to with OK signal.

Preface to further signal
Diver points to himself before giving a further signal, eg pointing to eyes to show you are to watch what he is about to do.

Dodgy signal
Something is wrong. May be followed by signal to ascend or indication of what is wrong, eg unable to equalise pressure on ears (points to ears). The dodgy signal is a flat hand, palm facing downwards, pivoted left to right and back a few times.

No more air
Diver points repeatedly with urgency to mouthpiece with cupped hand. He may require to share air, he may do an emergency ascent. Be alert and immediately hold on to him and commence air-sharing procedure. If he carries out an emergency ascent, follow immediately at normal ascent rate ready to give assistance at surface.

Cannot operate reserve lever
Clenched fist, arm bent at elbow holding fist at waist level followed by arm straightened and clenched fist lowered to thigh level. Sequence is repeated. This indicates that he cannot operate his reserve lever. Buddy should check the reserve rod immediately and be ready to share air if necessary.

On reserve
Clenched fist held level and parallel with mask. Indicates he is already on his reserve of air and will want to ascend immediately.

Stop. Stay where you are
Flat hand held up, palm towards you. Stop immediately. This will possibly be followed by another signal, indicating reason, unless it is obvious.

Distress
Clenched fist waved to and fro quickly, urgently. Assistance required immediately. Act calmly but quickly.

Out of breath
Both hands held to ribs, sometimes followed by a slowing down signal with arm. Indicates your buddy is out of breath and either wants to rest or swim more slowly.

OK and distress signals at surface
These are the same as already described; OK signal is given with arm outstretched above head to show boat cover you are OK but ready to be picked up. Distress signal is given with clenched fist by waving outstretched arm from side to side indicating that immediate assistance is required.

Danger
May follow stop signal. Finger drawn across throat and pointed to source of danger.

Signals should be given clearly and acknowledged in the same way. Never act on a signal you have given if you have not received an acknowledgement from your buddy. You may have signalled you intend going in one direction but if he has not seen the signal you will lose each other very quickly.

10
Life-jackets and Ascent Procedures

Life-jackets

There is no excuse for not wearing a suitable life-jacket when diving. Certainly they are not cheap but if trying to economise it is far better to do so in some other way. For instance, look out for a good secondhand cylinder instead of buying a shiny new one. It is also possible to find demand valves to purchase secondhand but make sure they are properly checked and serviced before you buy. You may be lucky enough to buy a good wetsuit secondhand.

Basically, there are two types of life-jacket although there are variations in styles, and changes are taking place all the time in all diving equipment.

Surface life-jacket

The surface life-jacket (SLJ) is inflated by means of a non-breathable gas cartridge. This contains enough gas to fill the jacket completely on the surface of the water. However, at 30m its volume and buoyancy will be about 25 per cent of that at the surface. Therefore, at this depth the average diver would be negatively buoyant with a fully inflated SLJ, unless he dropped his weightbelt. Even so, the rest of his equipment might anchor him to the seabed. It seems then that the SLJ, while ideal for surface sports, is not ideal for a diver although it is better than nothing. It is possible to purchase conversion kits with which to turn an SLJ into an ABLJ. If you decide to purchase an SLJ while you are snorkelling, you can, when the time is right, purchase such a kit rather than going to the expense of changing it for an ABLJ.

Assisted buoyancy life-jacket

The assisted buoyancy life-jacket (ABLJ) can bring a diver up from a maximum of 50m which is sufficient for the majority of sport divers should they get into trouble. Of course, this is only if the cylinder on the jacket is full. If you are, as are most divers, in the habit of using the jacket for buoyancy control underwater, then you will have used some of the air from the cylinder already. The ABLJ should only be used to assist ascent in real emergencies as there are inherent dangers in so doing. The life-jacket will jet a diver to the surface far more quickly than the normal safe ascent rate. There is a risk of embolism and/or decompression sickness depending on the situation.

All ABLJs are fitted with a relief valve for releasing excess air so that the jacket cannot over-inflate. There is also a dump valve for emptying the jacket or partially doing so. Integral with the hose should also be a valve which enables the diver to breathe from the jacket in an unusual emergency. He can also use the valve to inflate the jacket orally on the surface.

The ABLJ is fitted with a small bottle which can be refilled from a standard aqualung cylinder and this provides the air for inflation (or for the breathing in emergencies). Alternatively, there is the direct feed system. This entails a hose from an outlet on the first stage of the regulator by the pressure gauge hose outlet. This hose connects to the life-jacket and feeds air directly to it from the main cylinder on demand. It is an easy matter to convert a standard ABLJ to one which works from a direct feed. At the same time you can retain the cylinder on the jacket as an alternative means of air supply.

Instruction in the use of different types of ABLJ will be necessary and before using an ABLJ underwater a diver must undergo pool training along the following lines:

1 Practise swimming on the surface wearing an inflated ABLJ. You will find that it will impede progress if too full.
2 Enter the pool wearing normal equipment including aqualung. Practise surfacing drill then inflate on the surface. Practise inflating by mouth as well as with the bottle. Deflate the jacket by mouth using the automatic mouthpiece.
3 Walk into the pool, do not jump, wearing excess weight. Adjust buoyancy underwater by slowly leaking air into the jacket from the bottle. Do not fill more than is necessary to balance the excess weight. Vent air completely on bottom of pool. Swim to surface and inflate jacket.
4 Sit in shallow water just covering the head. Use extra weight to keep you on the bottom. Release a small amount of air into the jacket, breathe in air from jacket via the automatic mouthpiece. Breathe out through nose. Release more air into the jacket and repeat the breathing exercises until the air is used up. This exercise should be carried out under supervision.

Remember
1 Always charge the life-jacket bottle before every dive. Do not think it probably contains enough air as you cannot remember having used much last time you dived. You probably used more than you think on buoyancy control. This time it could be required for an emergency.
2 When using for buoyancy control, do so once only and you should be correctly buoyant for the rest of the dive. Do not waste air by constantly adjusting it with minor variations of depth.
3 If the life-jacket has been used to adjust buoyancy on the seabed remember to vent off the air before or during ascent. When using underwater ensure that the tap is firmly turned off after use. If you fail to do so air can gradually leak into the jacket during the dive. You may find yourself suddenly rising without warning. If this should happen, breathe out hard while simultaneously venting off the jacket. As you start to

descend again make sure the tap is firmly turned off.

4 Never use the life-jacket to assist your ascent except in a real emergency, eg severe cramp, malfunction of demand valve, etc. In this case *exhale forcibly and continuously on ascent*, as if whistling. Tilt your head back so that you are looking up towards the surface.

5 Don the life-jacket before the cylinder and weightbelt. You must be able to jettison gear while retaining the life-jacket.

6 To conserve the air in the life-jacket cylinder, inflate the jacket on the surface by mouth. If it is very rough, or in an emergency, use the bottle or direct feed.

Ascent procedures

The safe way to ascend should be practised in the pool before going in to the open sea. It should be carried out wearing full equipment. However, the same dangers exist with practice emergency ascents as with the real thing, therefore these are not undertaken in the sea.

Normal ascent
Assuming you have reached the level of air where you need to ascend, exchange the 'going' up signal with your buddy. Fin upwards at the rate of 20m a minute or at the rate of the small exhaust bubbles rising above you. Breathe normally at all times. *Do not hold your breath.* Watch your buddy, in poor visibility you should maintain physical contact. About two metres below the surface, pause and listen, turning through 360°. The sound of an engine will warn you of a nearby boat; look up as you turn. Assuming all is clear, continue ascent holding one hand above the head. On surfacing, turn full circle once more to check for nearby boats. Exchange OK signals with buddy and boat cover.

Assisted ascent (or buddy breathing)
Your buddy may give you the out-of-air signal. He will remain

stationary and you should go to him without delay, grasp his harness to maintain contact, and pass him your demand valve, having first taken air yourself. Make sure you pass it to him having pressed the purge button so that he receives a clear mouthpiece. He may not have sufficient breath in his lungs to expel water. He will then take two breaths and return the mouthpiece to you. You and your buddy should continue to take two breaths each until a regular rhythm is established. This being the case you exchange 'ascend' signals and fin gently upwards, maintaining air sharing.

During ascent *exhale slowly* when not in possession of the mouthpiece to avoid danger of air embolism. Continue to hold on to your buddy's harness. Watch the bubbles above to ensure safe ascent rate. You will also have to watch that you do not remain static or even descend without realising it. Make sure you both keep finning enough to maintain ascent.

Watch your buddy to ensure he is breathing out when necessary. If he is not press him in the region of the diaphragm to remind him to do so. Should he be feeling a bit panicky and breathless, you will have to allow him more breaths in relation to the breaths you take yourself.

If practising in the open sea this should only take place with two divers who dive regularly together and have carried out exhaustive practice in the pool beforehand.

Remember
1 Exhale slowly on ascent when not in possession of the mouthpiece.
2 Make sure your buddy is breathing out when necessary.
3 Maintain safe ascent rate.
4 If using twin hose regulator the donor diver should be slightly below the level of the distressed diver. This will ensure dependable airflow and exhaust.

Free ascent
Under no circumstances should this be practised in the open

103

sea. It is more dangerous than the real thing.

If you should be the one to be without air you may decide to undertake a free ascent. If you are diving with someone untrained or inexperienced in buddy breathing it may be preferable. Free ascent does increase the risk of a burst lung; in the case of a deep dive over the time limit it will also increase the possibility of decompression sickness.

Having found you are not getting air on demand you will immediately fin upwards. Remove the mouthpiece and exhale gently and continuously through pursed lips (as if whistling). Do not exceed a rate of more than 30m a minute. As you ascend, particularly in the last 10m, slow the rate of your ascent. Breathe out with more force at this time to reduce the risk of embolism.

Remember
1 Breathe out continuously.
2 In the last 10m particularly, slow to normal ascent rate.
3 Breathe out forcefully as you ascend to shallower water.

In extreme circumstances, if you are not rising you may have to ditch your weightbelt. This should not be necessary if you are wearing a life-jacket (see Buoyant Ascent in the following section).

If your buddy should carry out a free or buoyant ascent, follow him without delay but at the normal ascent rate. Do not put yourself at risk, he may require your assistance on or close to the surface.

Buoyant ascent
An alternative to free ascent if the diver, as he should be, is wearing a life-jacket (ABLJ). It carries the same risks as a free ascent but the possibility of embolism is increased. An ABLJ will only be used for underwater buoyancy control after rigorous training in the pool.

Do not release your weightbelt. Vent air into the ABLJ. As

you start to rise fin steadily and turn off the tap firmly (make sure air does not continue to leak into the jacket). Lean head back and breathe out forcefully. Watch for the surface.

Remember
1 Do not release your weightbelt.
2 Breathe out forcefully for the whole of the ascent to keep the volume of air in the lungs as low as possible.
3 Only use this method in a real emergency.

11
Aqualung Diving
in the Sea

At last, you are ready to use the aqualung in the sea. The first two or three dives using an aqualung are viewed by most with a mixture of excitement and slight apprehension. You will have become reasonably at home in the sea during your snorkelling dives. The slight apprehension you now feel is a healthy safety factor. No novice should be over-confident in his or her ability. This can lead to carelessness and possible dangers.

Water entry

If entering from the shore a gently sloping sand or shingle beach will be chosen as this gives the easiest entry. You can then don fins at the edge of the water and walk slowly backwards until it is deep enough for you to turn and swim. A site within a reasonable snorkel swim will be chosen and your instructor will ensure you both surface with sufficient air to be able to swim back using the aqualung if this should be necessary.

Entry from a boat is an easy way to start a dive, there being no long swim involved. Having checked and donned all gear you seat yourself on the tubes or gunwales of the boat. Check the water behind you to ensure all is clear. Holding one hand over your mask and demand valve, one on your cylinder harness, tuck your head forwards. Relax and roll backwards over the side. You will submerge only a short depth and will bob up again immediately like a cork. Continue to breathe normally during your water entry and submersion. Having surfaced, signal OK to the boat handler and to your instructor who will have entered the water before you and will be waiting on the surface. He will then give the signal to dive. Make sure your mask strap is properly in place and that you are ready to dive before returning the signal. You should also check your buoyancy before diving.

Whether you go from shore or boat, when you use an aqualung there is a common minor problem which besets numerous new divers. Due to the slight anxiety you may feel, you breathe more quickly. This leads to a build-up of air in the lungs. This in turn makes you more buoyant and you find it difficult to descend. You are usually unaware that this is happening and are convinced you are underweighted, despite having already checked your buoyancy. The simple answer is to settle yourself down on the surface by breathing regularly. Do not take a huge breath before duck diving beneath, just continue to breathe normally. You will have learnt from your snorkelling experience that huge breaths of air are not necessary even without an aqualung. A good instructor will assist you to relax at the surface.

To instil confidence through personal contact he will hold your hand or arm as you descend and possibly during the first dive. Throughout all your training never be too proud to admit that something concerns you. The sooner you admit it the more quickly you can be helped in overcoming the problem.

Descent

The most common way to leave the surface is by using the duck dive to get underwater. Having dived you can turn right side up and drop feet first. The deeper you go the less buoyant you will be and therefore will drop quite easily. Your instructor will watch your eyes for sign of any discomfort and be alert for any signal that you are unable to 'clear' your ears. If you do not return his OK signals he will halt the descent and may signal you to return with him to the surface. This is a safety measure in case of equalising problems or a possible build-up of discomfort which can easily be overcome with a little encouragement.

As you descend concentrate on clearing your ears and relaxing. Breathe normally. Relieve any pressure on your face mask by a snort of air down the nose. If you do experience difficulty in 'clearing' then signal your instructor. Also watch his signals to you, and return them.

Descending feet first makes it easier to deal with equalisation of pressure on mask and ears. A number of divers prefer to swim head first to the seabed, particularly during deep dives. Time then is at a premium and it is normal to swim down the anchor line as quickly as is safe, to ensure maximum time on the seabed.

An alternative way of leaving the surface is by relaxing and exhaling heavily. By almost emptying your lungs you lose buoyancy and drop underwater easily. You continue to drop feet first to the seabed in the normal way.

On the seabed

Your first few dives will probably take place in 10m of water or less. Having reached the seabed settle yourself in your gear. Compression of your suit may mean that your weightbelt and cylinder harness are sloppy. Adjust these to fit snugly. A weightbelt hanging loose on your hips and/or a cylinder moving excessively on your back can be distracting. After a few dives these minor adjustments will become automatic and will only take seconds.

Before the dive your instructor will have told you on which side of him he would like you to swim. Make sure you do swim beside and not above him. Do not suddenly swim off at a tangent to look at something without exchanging signals. In a few fin strokes you could be lost to view. You will, in any case, probably be held in the vice-like grip of your instructor who does not want to lose you. Alternatively, you will be holding the buoy-line to ensure constant contact between you. Get into the habit of checking your pressure gauge to keep an eye on the contents of your cylinder. Likewise check your depth gauge occasionally. This will be most important when you are diving in deeper water.

You will have learned all the basic signals but there are numerous ways of communicating underwater. When diving regularly you will get used to these. If you get cold, signal by hugging your body and simulating shivering. Do not wait until you are so cold you cannot concentrate. If you feel sick, or so uncomfortable you want to surface; give the 'dodgy' signal. If you feel out of breath, signal to slow down.

Ascent

When you are down to 30atm you should signal your instructor and he will then signal to ascend with you. If using a reserve valve on your cylinder then signal when you pull the reserve. Irrespective of how much more air the instructor has left he will surface at the same time. Go up at the rate of approximately 20m a minute. Never overtake your bubbles. Breathe normally. *Do not* hold your breath at any time. About two metres from the surface pause, listen for boat engines, looking up and turning through 360°. This is to ensure you do not surface under a boat. Assuming it is safe, continue ascent holding one arm outstretched above your head. On reaching the surface, by the marker buoy, again turn through 360° and give the OK signal to boat cover and instructor.

On the surface

During the first two or three dives you will wear a life-jacket for use only on the surface. There is a fair amount of training involved in the use of one for buoyancy control underwater. This usually takes place after you have had an opportunity to use all your other equipment in the sea. When you have reached the surface and signalled you then inflate your life-jacket. Do not fill it completely but merely enough to keep your head above the water. If it is calm you can fill it by mouth. If choppy, it is advisable to fill it by means of the bottle. Providing the boat handler has seen you and is able to come and pick you up, stay where you have surfaced. Never swim towards a moving boat. The boat handler is judging his speed and direction to pick you up at your point of surfacing. He also, particularly with an inflatable, has to take into consideration the direction and force of the wind. He will be judging his approach so that he can reach you as the propeller stops turning. You can relax in the water on your life-jacket but watch the boat until it is alongside. Also be aware of the movements of any other boats in the area.

At the boat, hold the ropes along the tubes (or the ladder or fender if a hard boat). When someone is ready, hand in your weightbelt, followed by the cylinder. Entry into an inflatable is easy but takes a bit of practice. Holding the ropes use your fins underwater to give you some propulsion. As you rise out of the water straighten your arms and lean forward over the tubes. Your top half should now be far enough into the boat to enable you to swing your legs in easily. Remember there will be other divers in the boat so avoid hitting them with your fins.

On the boat

The boat handler is in charge of dropping and picking up divers. He has the responsibility of looking after you. Do not enter or leave the boat without his signal.

Try and keep your gear up together as much as possible. On a hard boat this will be fairly easy as you will be able to take your diving bag aboard. On an inflatable or dory room is restricted and the ride can be fairly bumpy so that all efforts to keep gear together may fail dismally. Wear life-jacket, compass, etc. If the practice with the group is to go fully kitted then you must comply. Never wear your weightbelt unless you are also going to be wearing your fins.

Remember

Your instructor will help you learn to dive safely. He will do what he can to teach you. He will look after you on your first sea dives. However, to become a good diver you have to take responsibility for yourself. You can only do this by listening, remembering, watching and learning. If you are not interested enough to learn then you should not be diving at all and will be a danger to yourself and other people. Diving is a practical sport. Show you have commonsense and enthusiasm and you will find other divers quite happy to help you learn.

Always check your gear before leaving for the dive. Make sure that you are not the type of diver who is always borrowing from others.

Simple underwater navigation

A diver can easily become disorientated underwater, particularly in very poor visibility where there is no lighter water above to indicate the surface. In exceptionally good visibility where the water above and below the diver is equally crystal clear and the seabed is not visible, he may feel something akin to mild vertigo, a sensation of falling, but this will quickly pass.

The reason for this loss of direction or position is that the diver depends almost entirely on visual aids. The sun on the water above indicates the surface. His bubbles rising towards it mean he is right side up. Very poor visibility or diving in the dark takes away both these indicators.

Most divers with experience navigate underwater, in reasonable visibility, by following the lie of the seabed and noting tide patterns in the sand. 'Landmarks' such as a large boulder, etc, also help. At the same time the depth gauge keeps the diver within his planned depth and the compass enables him to go in the required direction and, if planned, to return to the original area of entry.

Entry into the water must be made at a point fixed as

accurately as possible. A vague notion of it being the right spot is not good enough and a diver can spend many a wasted dive trying to find the reef, wreck or lost trawler dredge. If called in to find a lost object it will probably be a pointless exercise unless the fisherman or other person has taken proper bearings with which to mark the search areas. Better still if he has dropped a marker buoy.

There are several methods of searching underwater. By means of rope or wire grids or squares or by using a central stake and carrying out a circular sweep. The first two methods are used by those wishing to make a thorough and careful search for an item or items, as in the excavation of a shipwreck. If searching for a lost anchor or similar the common practice is to first put down the anchor line at the spot. The diver follows the line down for a quick reconnaisance dive (providing the depth allows him time). He then takes down a line which he attaches in the area of the anchor to use for a circular sweep.

The compass is essential for every diver, whatever the depth or area. It should be worn strapped to the wrist alone, not right next to a watch which will affect its accuracy. Hold the compass directly ahead of the central line of travel at eye level. Make sure your head and body are in line and that you do not inadvertently turn your head and arm out of alignment. This will put you off course. Tidal pull or one leg stronger than the other can also affect your course. Once in the sea, take a bearing from a point on shore or, if the boat is to remain anchored, this can be used from which to take a bearing.

If searching for a lost item, once found, attach a marker buoy. Once back on the surface you may never find it again. If it is not too heavy you can use your life-jacket to help lift the item to the surface. This can be risky and should not be attempted by a novice.

Shore diving

To build up stamina and experience shore dives are ideal. The exercise, which is so good for you, starts with getting the gear down to the water's edge. Before you reach that stage though, the right amount of organisation will mean that your outing is successful.

First, decide when and where you would like to dive. Bear in mind the ease with which you can get into the water, and out again. Also how far it will be from car to water's edge; the gear always seems that much heavier on the way back when you are tired and possibly a bit chilled. If possible, choose a sandy beach which has a very gentle incline. Pebble beaches can be a little more difficult as they shelve quite sharply and you may have to contend with a bit of surf pulling at you as you walk in, slightly top-heavy with equipment and ungainly in fins. Climbing over slippery rocks with heavy gear is definitely to be avoided.

Having decided where, you must check the weather conditions and the state of the tide, not only when leaving but when you are likely to come ashore. Check locally for any strong currents and their behaviour in relation to the state of the tide. If you do get caught in a current never try to swim against it. Swim across it diagonally until you are eventually out of its pull.

Do not dive in fairways or shipping channels. Choose a site which is not too far from land, particularly when you are just learning to dive and have not properly tested your stamina, or your abilities. As you will be diving fairly close to shore avoid areas likely to be infested with high-powered speedboats, particularly those hired out to inexperienced holidaymakers.

Before leaving, advise someone on shore what your intentions are and your approximate time of return. Try and have someone on the beach as a shore cover. A counsel of perfection is also to have snorkel cover but this is not always possible unless you are diving with a large club. Make sure you are towing a buoy, preferably the type with a diving flag on the top. Aim to finish the dive with some air left for emergencies. You may feel perfectly fit and able to snorkel all the way back to land but you have to allow for the unexpected at sea.

If you find you will have to come ashore in surf do not stand up and try to walk through it. It is better to swim as far as possible, until you are actually lying on the sand and only in the wash of the water, rather than the weight of the breakers. Then it is possible to roll over and remove fins before standing up. This, of course, only works on a sandy beach. Coming ashore in surf on a sharp pebble incline can be difficult and should be avoided if at all possible. This can be helped by planning the dive so that the surf is at its least hectic, ie the tide will be in such a position as to be coming in against the more gently shelving land further out rather than at full spate against the sharpest point of the beach.

Snorkelling in open water
1 Do not go too far from land until you have had an opportunity to assess your stamina, and that of your buddy.
2 Make enquiries about the state and effect of the tides in the area.
3 Organise the dive so that you are able to return to shore near to where you entered.
4 Always tow a marker buoy so that boats know there is something under the surface. A buoy with a diving flag on the top is particularly good.
5 Always wear a diving knife when in open water.
6 Do not dive in fairways, busy shipping channels or areas where there are numerous speedboats in use.
7 Tell someone on shore before you go and how long you intend to be away.
8 Wear a surface life-jacket. If you do unknowingly overstretch yourself you will have a support on which to rest.
9 If you are overtired and are not wearing a life-jacket, ditch your weightbelt to make the journey back less of an effort.

12
Use of Boats,
Charts and Tides

As far as diving is concerned the best small boat on the market must be the inflatable. The majority of boat-owning divers use them, although it must be said that dories are becoming increasingly popular. The inflatable is easy to transport on land and suits the wanderings of the diver as he searches for new places from which to dive. It is virtually unsinkable if properly used. Being constructed with compartments of rubber filled with air, if one compartment should spring a leak then the others will not be affected. Its stability in the water makes it ideal, it scarcely heels when a diver falls into the water or clambers back wearing heavy equipment. They come in various sizes costing from several hundred to several thousand pounds and, therefore, something is available to suit most pockets. According to their size and construction they carry a variety of sizes of outboard engines.

Only by investigating the various types of boat which are on the market, and by talking to clubs and other boatowners, can you eventually find the one which is right for your diving. As with all diving gear, never be tempted to buy something which is cheap simply for that reason. Better to spend more money on something which is safe and which is going to last.

You will often see boats or engines for sale secondhand. This can be a good way of buying if you are a bit short of cash. The life of an inflatable is about ten years (or diving seasons). The action of the sea plus the wear it receives from carrying heavy

115

gear means that the rubber will gradually become porous. Great care should be taken when purchasing an engine secondhand. As with a car engine, a lot depends on the previous owner and the way he maintained and used it. If you do not know anything about engines it is best to have it inspected by an expert.

Boat capacity

The points governing your choice will be the type of diving you intend pursuing and how many divers will generally make up the party. If you will be diving close to shore, say, within a mile, then you could get away with a 3–4m boat with an 8–10hp engine. If you want to be more flexible and will normally carry up to six divers, then you will need 5m as a minimum for comfort as well as safety. At the least a 20hp engine will be needed. Apart from the divers you have to bear in mind the diving equipment and boat equipment which will be carried. Estimate the maximum load she is ever likely to carry and then add 20 per cent. This will give you a guide to the load-carrying capacity your boat will need.

Transportation

In theory you purchase the inflatable because it can be deflated. In practice it very rarely is, mainly because it first has to be washed down carefully with fresh water and every bit of sand, seaweed, grit, etc, has to be removed. The following trip it has to be reinflated, either by footpump (tiring and time-consuming) or via a connection from an air cylinder (a waste of air you could use underwater). Therefore, boat and engine are usually given a quick wash off with fresh water and left until the following dive.

A small inflatable can be carried on the roof of a car. For the larger one there is a wide choice of trailer available. These divide into two categories. The low boat trailer can carry boat with engine attached and can be pulled right down the slipway or beach into the water where the boat is unloaded. The other type is the box trailer, a heavier trailer which can be fitted with an immersible chassis. As its name suggests it is like a box without a top and is ideal for carrying the engine, cylinders, weightbelts, etc, with the boat strapped on the top. For those who already have a car full of camping gear, or for those wishing to keep wet diving equipment out of the shining car, a box trailer is probably the answer.

Care of engine

It should be stressed that an engine should be properly maintained. There are courses available which will tell you how to do a lot of the work yourself. Maintenance is better than repairs – these are always expensive on an outboard engine. Proper care helps to avoid breakdowns, these always seem to occur a long way from land. When carrying the engine in the trailer, make sure it is properly cushioned from the jolting of bad road surfaces with thick foam or an old tyre.

Boat equipment

The anchor is the most important piece of equipment. It should be readily stowable and easily available in emergencies. It has to be suitable for all types of seabed and be able to hold the boat in roughish sea and strong winds. It is not just for throwing down in shallow water in a flat calm sea. You need an anchor for all seasons, probably with a starting weight of around 10kg. Of all the anchors available the most useful are the CQR or the Darnforth anchor. Both of these stow well in a small boat. A short length of chain attached to the anchor will help prevent the anchor from pulling out of the seabed. There will be more strain put on the anchor if tied directly to line whereas the chain will lie along the seabed. Nylon or terylene line is usually used now, it is strong, durable and has a certain amount of give in it.

When anchoring you have to allow enough line for a minimum of twice the depth of water beneath you, plus some spare.

Paddles or oars are a necessity. Outboard engines seem to have phases of breaking down. In a loaded boat you will find paddles easier to use than oars as no rowlocks are required. Also in connection with breakdowns, or other emergencies, flares should always be carried in the boat kit. These should never be fired unless it is a real emergency. Also, you must be sure that someone is going to see it – other boats, coastguard station, etc.

A diving flag must be flown when divers are in the water. You have to let other boats know, in the hope that they will avoid the area. This is especially important when the other boat-users are the inexperienced hired-for-an-hour speedboat types which plague some areas of coastline. If you are sensible you will keep away from these areas altogether.

A boat kit containing various spares, patches, etc, should be carried in a watertight container for use on land or at sea. This must be checked regularly as spares have a habit of disappearing just when you need them. A first aid kit for humans should also be carried. A bailer and bellows or foot pump should be carried as a matter of course. With an inflatable you may find you have a soft compartment in one of the tubes due to a tiny leak. If you are out for a longish spell at sea when this is discovered it is a comfort to be able to keep air pumped into it, especially when you have a boat full of divers.

Launching the boat

Obviously the easiest place to launch is a slipway or jetty. More and more, as the search for new sites continues, divers are having to launch from the beach. Wherever you choose as your launching site, make sure that your trailer does not impede the access for other people. Likewise, try and keep your diving gear as tidy as possible, not strewn along harbour walls or across car parks. Wherever you intend to launch, you will have to bear in mind the distance the boat may have to be carried without the aid of a trailer. Also how many bodies you have to assist you.

Learning to handle a boat is like learning to drive a car. It can only be carried out properly under the supervision of someone who is experienced. It is not something you can learn from a book, although this can give you a few pointers on safety.

Handling the boat starts on the beach. It is not a very safe operation if there is anything other than a flat calm sea and no wind. In these circumstances one way is to get the boat and engine into the water leaving her bow held forward by one diver. All the gear is then loaded and the rest of the divers climb aboard, leaving the anchorman waist high in cold water. Once the engine is started and working you can allow him aboard. Always make sure the bow is kept pointing out to sea and that the engine is going before you are all aboard or, if anchored, before the anchor is pulled up.

When launching in surf more care is needed. It takes experience to judge when the right moment comes between waves to take the boat, bow-first, out through the breakers to the calmer water. In these conditions it is safest to put out an anchor line in case engine trouble develops. The engine must be started up as quickly as possible and taken away from the divers. The handler then waits on the anchor for the gear to be loaded. This can sometimes mean the divers kitting up and swimming out to the boat. If there is a bit of swell or slight chop then it may be necessary to keep the engine running so that the bow can take the force of the waves but this is to be avoided if possible as it increases the danger to the divers in the water. Unless the boat can be launched with the minimum risk to all parties it is best to abandon the dive or look for a safer site.

Do not overload the boat. Also be careful in the stowing of the heavy gear, particularly if there is a choppy sea. The weather conditions could worsen while you are out and a wrongly-loaded boat could be swamped. If you are taking a boat handler who is not diving, make sure he has his mask, fins and snorkel with him in case of emergencies.

The boat and the divers

An inflatable when not being propelled by its engine can be blown helplessly by the wind, or even a stiff breeze. If you are in charge of the boat for this dive then insist on buoys being used by the divers and keep a close eye on them. If an emergency does arise you must be on hand to pick them up quickly.

When retrieving a diver you must come up to him against the wind, but with the tide. This means he is not getting taken away from you. Arrive so that he is able to grasp one of the ropes along the side. Gauge your arrival so that the engine is out of gear and, if possible, the screw has stopped turning before you actually come alongside the diver. Every care has to be taken in this as a turning propeller can inflict nasty damage on a diver. Do not allow yourself to be distracted, keep your eye on him all the time. Other divers on the boat can take his cylinder and weightbelt. If you are alone then you must make sure the engine remains running but in neutral while you take his equipment.

Anchoring at sea

You may want to anchor over a wreck or reef site and have lined up the marks. You have the exact spot, you believe. Before going any further make sure that you have one end of the anchor line secured to the boat. It should be kept secured at all times as it has been known, on more than one occasion, for an enthusiastic novice to fling anchor and line overboard to disappear for ever. So, keep it secured, line neatly coiled and ready for use, not a messy tangle somewhere forward under two cylinders. It is also a good idea to keep a small buoy tied to the line. If an emergency arises you can then untie the line from the boat and throw it overboard, marked by the buoy for easy recovery. This saves a distressed diver waiting while you fiddle about trying to release an anchor which has become firmly embedded in part of the wreck.

If you want to follow the anchor line down then you must, as far as possible, make sure you drop the anchor into the site at the right point. Stop the boat, heading into the wind, or against the tide, whichever is strongest at the time. Drop the anchor and go astern gently, paying out the anchor line smoothly. Do not just heave the whole thing over the side, you will have to haul the resulting mess up and start all over again. By then you will have lost the site. Knowing the approximate depth of the water, pay out twice as much line.

Three knots which are most commonly used in connection with boats are illustrated in Fig 22. The reef knot is used to join

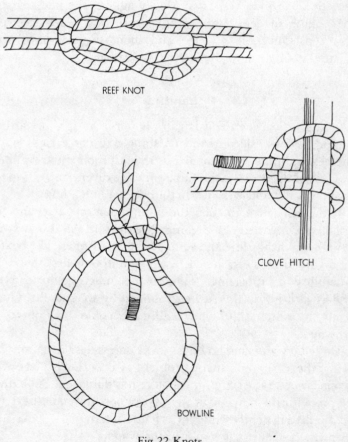

REEF KNOT

CLOVE HITCH

BOWLINE

Fig 22 Knots

two pieces of rope of equal thickness. The bowline is used when a non-slip loop is required. The clove hitch is commonly used for securing a line – it is quick, easy and it works.

Berthing

Coming in to land at a jetty takes skill if you are to avoid scratching the precious rubber of the inflatable. Make sure both bowline and sternline are ready for use. Head towards the jetty, trying to keep parallel with it. Allow for the strength and direction of wind. Make way slowly against the tide, keeping the engine in gear and working until you reach the spot required. Once the bowline and then sternline have been secured you can stop the engine altogether.

Landing

Landing on a beach if it is calm is fairly straightforward. It should be possible on sand or shingle to come right up to the beach, lifting the propeller at the last moment and gliding the rest of the way. At the same time the divers leap out in the shallow water and assist her to the edge for unloading.

If the sea is rough then the boat should stay beyond the breakers with the engine going. Meanwhile the divers swim in with an anchor line and some of the heavy gear. The boat is then guided in, stern first. If it is taken in bow first there is a possibility of capsizing. The boat handler could end up underneath her in the surf surrounded by weightbelts. Quite funny to watch until you realise he could be injured or drowned.

Do not try and land amongst rocks unless it is flat calm. This being the case your main problem is ensuring you get the propeller up at the right time, before it is damaged. Put a diver ashore with the bowline at the first opportunity and have the boat pulled in gently while she is fended off from the rocks, and with the propeller safely out of the water.

When beaching, never put a diver out of the boat into the water unless he is wearing mask, fins and snorkel, except when you are sure beyond any doubt, that the depth of the water is less than waist height.

Weather

As a diver you become far more aware of the direction and force of the wind. It is the wind which really dictates where and when you will dive. Of course other factors play a part but it is the wind which has most effect on the state of the sea. It dictates whether it will be rough or calm. You can save many a wasted trip if you learn to read how it is likely to affect the sites at which you intend to dive. Thus you may change to another part of the coast where the wind does not have an adverse effect. As a very rough guide, if it is blowing offshore, ie from land to sea, depending on its force, then the sea should not be too rough. If it is blowing from the sea towards the shore or, in some areas, along shore, then you are likely to find it too rough for launching a boat.

The state of wind is not only important on the day on which you wish to dive. You should also note its condition during the previous few days. If the wind is only starting to blow up on the day you dive you may be lucky. Local enquiries should be made to avoid getting out to sea and halfway through a dive when it really starts to get rough. If the wind has been blowing fairly steadily for a few days you will find that the sea is already too lumpy for a small boat. Likewise it may be too hazardous for a 'hard' boat to drop and retrieve divers.

Certain winds can set up a ground swell which lasts for days and reduces visibility to zero. The sea may appear to be almost calm, the sky bright blue and the sun shining but beneath the water it will probably be as black as night.

If planning a dive near an estuary it is commonsense to avoid the area if there has been torrential rain. This washes mud down the river and out into the sea, the visibility being nil for days afterwards. Obviously you do not dive where the sea is crashing on to the beach and the water is the colour of tea.

The weather is something you learn to read over a period of time. As with anything the key to being a good diver is being prepared to listen and learn. Seasoned divers can be a great help to you in getting to know where and when to dive. For local knowledge the fishermen are certainly the best people to consult.

Water movement

Waves are, broadly, a result of the action of the wind. Its force, the period of time it is at that strength, and the distance over which it is acting produces a swell. This swell travels as a series of waves. A set of larger waves followed by a lull of smaller ones. It will be seen that the more open the site, and the stronger the onshore wind, the rougher will be the sea in that area.

Waves moving towards land are reduced in speed by the shallower waters of the seabed. This decrease shortens the length of the wave (the distance from the crest of one wave to the crest of the one following). The wave is forced upward. It becomes steeper and less stable. When the height of the wave is slightly exceeded by the depth of the water, the wave will break.

Difficulty can be experienced by a diver trying to enter the sea from a steep beach. The wave breaks and washes up the slope. It then washes back to flow under the next incoming wave. This surging action can be difficult to stand up against.

If diving in fairly shallow water some effects can be felt if the swell is large. An underwater surge is caused and this can carry the diver. It is fairly rare but does often happen when diving too close to a rocky coastline or between a rocky coast and reef. Great care should be taken in the choice of site. It has been known for a powerful surge to push a diver up to the surface through several metres of water. He was in motion so quickly that he was unable to readjust his buoyancy. The air in his jacket expanded during ascent and, of course, hastened him on his way. That was an extreme case which ended with no harm done – he had the presence of mind to breathe out hard on the journey up while trying to vent off the air in his jacket.

Thermocline

This is the term used for a sudden change in water temperature within a body of water. This can be felt when descending, as you pass through a 'layer' of water which is suddenly colder and then goes up in temperature a few metres further down.

Generally speaking the difference in temperature when entering a thermocline will only be a few degrees warmer or colder. It can be enough though to affect the type of life which inhabits that layer of water. There are also seasonal reasons for thermoclines, particularly in hot climates where the temperature of the surface metres of water can be affected.

Tides

Apart from weather the state of the tide governs when you will be able to dive. To enable you to calculate these times it is necessary to acquire knowledge of the behaviour of the tides. There are a number of tide tables available for different parts of the coast and this information is also available in various nautical books. It is, of course, important to make sure you are using the tables for the current year.

Tides do not flow in and out but backwards and forwards along the coast. They are the alterations in the level of the sea in response to the forces of the moon and sun. These forces vary as the earth changes its position in relation to the moon and sun. In some parts of the world there is no change felt in the state of the tide.

Spring and neap tides
About one and a half days after new and full moon (or every fifteen days), the earth, moon and sun are nearly in line and the

greatest range of forces which result produce the highest and lowest levels of water. These are known as spring tides. The sea does not respond instantly to the tide-generating forces and this accounts for the one and a half day lapse. Approximately seven and a half days after spring tides the least gravitational pull is being exerted and the tides of lowest range are produced. These are referred to as neap tides. Between spring and neap tides there is a gradual decrease in the height of the tides.

In British waters there are two high and two low tides during a period of approximately twenty-four hours, the duration of the flow of tide being six hours twelve minutes. As a guide, the range of the tide is divided into twelfths spread over the six hours, as below.

1st hour one twelfth of tide flowing – slack water
2nd hour two twelfths
3rd hour three twelfths ⎫
4th hour three twelfths ⎬ most water flowing
5th hour two twelfths
6th hour one twelfth of tide flowing – slack water

The best time to dive is at slack water, ie when least water is flowing. This is usually within an hour before or after high or low water but the visibility could be better at slack water high. The tables will give the time of high tide and its maximum height so that you can estimate slack water high and add six hours and find approximate time of low water and thus slack water low. If using Greenwich Mean Time tables for British Summer Time you will have to add an hour in your calculations.

Tidal pulls vary enormously in different parts of the world as well as from place to place on a given coast. Although the tables give a good guide to times these local variations must be taken into consideration. Some slack water times, instead of being when expected, come up two hours after high or low water. When diving in sites unknown to you check with local fishermen to make sure you pick the best time to dive.

Charts and navigation – transit bearings

When discussing diving sites you will hear 'transit bearings' or 'marks' used (see Fig 23). Simply, these are the means by which a site can be found. At the site prominent landmarks are chosen which can be lined up with each other, eg a clump of trees, a church, perhaps a strangely-shaped hill or headland. To use these marks you should line them up until they are one behind the other. If you are too far away they will stand apart. As you progress towards them they line up. If you go too far they should 'pass' each other and become out of line once again. On paper this seems to be a rough and ready way of marking a spot but it does work, and it is free.

There are numerous aids to navigation and they range in price from a few pounds to a few hundreds. For a sport diver using an inflatable or dory there are perhaps two which may be useful. One is fairly cheap, the other varies in price according to

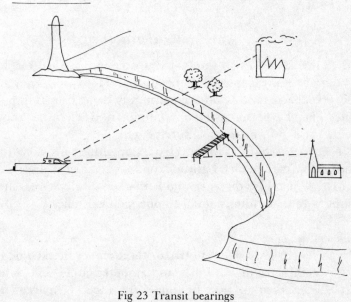

Fig 23 Transit bearings

type. Otherwise, transit bearings are the answer and one which fishermen have used successfully for hundreds of years – even though they are using rather more sophisticated aids these days.

Hand-bearing compass
This is still, even today, purchased at a fairly reasonable price. It is relatively simple to use. It enables you to take bearings from landmarks which can then be transferred to a chart. These bearings can then be used to give a position line.

Echo sounder
The simple type of sounder is a means of checking the depth of water beneath you. It is good for use in conjunction with transit bearings, for example when pin-pointing a reef, which can be difficult; the echo sounder gives you a means of checking the depth at any given point. Tidal variations have to be taken into account. Print-out sounders can be purchased but these are fairly expensive and unsuitable for use on a small boat.

Admiralty charts

When diving in British waters being able to make sense of an Admiralty chart helps you to move around the coast. They are the best charts to use and are constantly being brought up to date. They have been printed in fathoms and feet but are now being printed in metric measurements.

There are two scales on the chart. Longitude runs along top and bottom of the chart. Latitude runs down the sides. Latitude is used to measure distance and is marked off in degrees and minutes (one minute is equal to one nautical mile).

The compass rose
On each chart you will find two or three circles marked off in degrees, each having an inner and an outer circle. The outer circle is marked in true bearings, the inner is marked in

magnetic bearings. Across the rose is written variation, followed by degrees and minutes east or west and then a date in brackets. The annual decrease is also given in minutes. To find magnetic north this decrease must be taken into consideration. The allowance must be made from the year shown on the chart to the present day, then applied to true north.

Magnetic course
This is when true course is plotted on the chart and the variation is applied.

Deviation
This is the magnetic effect of the boat on the compass when on a specific bearing. If there is deviation then this should also be applied to the true course to find steering course.

Lowest astronomical tide
The lowest level of tide predicted ever to occur, at any time, in any conditions. Normally mean low water springs will be higher than this level.

Tidal streams
On the chart there are diamonds in each of which is a capital letter. They relate to sections in the panel marked tidal streams. These sections give information with regard to rate and direction of tidal streams hourly before and after high water at the point marked on the chart. Latitude and longitude of the sites of tide measurement are given at the top of the section. The name of a standard port to which the facts relate will be found at the side of the panel. If the tidal stream is given as northerly it means that the stream is flowing towards north.

To really understand how to use a chart to its full advantage, consult a manual such as *Reed's Nautical Almanac* or *Coastwise Navigation*. The information will be invaluable to you when looking for known sites or pin-pointing new ones for further investigation.

13
Underwater Interests

Underwater interests

Once you have reached a reasonable standard of proficiency you will probably want to spend your time underwater following a specific avenue which will add to your enjoyment. You will have your own ideas but will find it useful to talk to other divers of like mind. It is very irritating for both parties when diving if one wants to rush about not looking for anything except that which is edible and the other only wants to make a minute study of a particular type of seaweed. As with most things you will find those with similar interests tend to gravitate towards each other so you should have no trouble in finding a buddy with whom to dive.

Marine biology

During your early diving you will assimilate some information on the more commonly seen fish and plant life. Eventually, if you really wish to learn more about the world you are visiting, you will have to decide on what particular branch of life you wish to study. Marine biology is a vast subject and there are numerous books on the subject. It is really not easy to pick one branch from such an enormous range. However, if you do not specialise you will end up with a confused, if interesting, jumble of notes on fish, plant life, molluscs, etc, about which you find you know very little.

130

Having decided on the subject you will have to decide how to approach it, the specific points you wish to note. Visit the type of area on which you will find the specimens. Take a board or slate and pencil on which to record date, site of dive (with sketch map if possible), time of dive and state of tide. Visibility, depth range, type of seabed, water topography, general description of subject and measurements. If taking a specimen take only one, preferably take a photograph instead.

The notes you take will only be brief so make sure you transfer your information into a record book on the same day as the dive. Every detail will be fresh in your mind. Gradually you will build up a detailed picture of your chosen item.

If you intend taking a serious interest in marine biology find out about lectures held on the subject. Attend courses combined with diving expeditions which are run at different times of the year. Information on these courses can usually be obtained through a diving club or magazines. Keep one or two good books at home for reference purposes but generally libraries keep a selection for occasional reference.

Underwater photography

Underwater photography is a very rewarding extension to diving. By taking photographs you can record, in brilliantly true colours, all the enchantment of the life you see around you. It enables you to share your fascinating hobby, in a small way, with other people.

With a little experience it is possible to achieve some really good results. There are several simple-to-use cameras, both still and cine, which can be purchased at reasonable cost. Perspex housings can be bought for a considerable range of still and cine cameras, thereby enabling you to use a camera you may already own. Alternatively, some firms supply components with which to make a housing yourself. There are cameras on the market which can be used on land or underwater without any housing. Naturally your choice of camera is governed by the type of photography in which you are interested. If you just want a few snapshots as a record of your various diving expeditions then you will require one of the cheaper but easily operated cameras without housing. If you want to take the subject more seriously you will wish to research the subject thoroughly before purchasing.

Lenses

If you are able to afford a choice then a wide angle lens is best for underwater photography, giving brighter, clearer, sharper photographs. It allows you to get closer to your subject and eliminates scattering. Scattering is caused by suspended particles in the water which reflect light. The particles between you and the subject, plus the scattering of the light, cause a foggy effect. Your subject tends to merge into the background. The further you are from your subject the more the loss of definition increases. Even in quite clear water you are unlikely to get a really sharp picture over 3–5m. Photographing just below the surface or in mid-water rather than on the seabed helps eliminate the problem as the water is likely to be clearer. A close-up lens is a good investment, particularly if you are interested in the finer detail of the plant or fish life you may be photographing.

Refraction

The refraction of light affects your camera in the same way it affects your own vision. If a subject is actually 100cm away it will appear to be only 75cm. You should set your camera for the apparent distance, not the measured distance. Some lenses are designed for underwater use only. These see distances in the same way a normal lens would see distance on land.

Focusing

It is difficult to judge distance accurately underwater. It is a good idea to use a 75cm stick as a guide. Presetting the camera to the same distance and working within that field also helps.

Depth of field is the area sharply in focus from a point in front to a point behind the subject. The higher F number used, the greater the distance focused, eg F16 approx. 60–120cm, F2 approx. 80–100cm.

Shutter speeds
As a general rule it is best to use the lower shutter speeds, 1/60th or 1/30th second to allow use of F numbers which will give you a greater depth of focus. If using flash you will be restricted to setting the camera to the shutter speed which is correct for the type of flash.

Exposure
Learning the correct exposure rating will come after having taken a few films and noting which number is used for the conditions and type of film. A light meter is an advantage. Generally it should be tilted down towards the subject to avoid a false reading from the brighter surface above. However, it must be said, that when filming a subject on a very light sandy bottom in clear visibility the same care must be taken when tilting down as this type of seabed can have the same reflective qualities as snow.

Make a habit of recording all readings and conditions of visibility plus type of seabed on which to base further filming.

Loss of light and colour
The deeper you go the more light is absorbed. When the sun is at its height more light penetrates than during the morning or later afternoon. The best period during which to film is between noon and two o'clock. Weather conditions before and during the dive also affect underwater visibility. If it has been stormy for several days before the dive you may find the silt stirred up and the scattering of light intensified. Colours disappear underwater due to absorption. Red is the first to be filtered out followed by yellow. Depending on conditions and locality films can take on a green or blue tinge. This can be eliminated by the

use of the flash. If you are not using a flash, staying in shallow water (say, less than twenty metres) and using filters will help to combat the problem. Of course, if filming in the clear waters of the Caribbean you are not likely to have quite the same problems as if you are limited to British waters.

Flash

Using flash will reproduce the true colours of the subject. It enables you to use higher F numbers therefore giving greater depth of focus producing sharper pictures. You can also use fill-in flash for dark areas, such as highlighting a face within a mask.

There are two groups of flash: flash bulbs and electronic flash or strobe lights. Some of the cheaper cameras incorporate a bulb flash unit. A disadvantage of using bulbs is having to carry them with you and change them for each shot. Electronic flash requires a perspex housing but this is not necessarily a disadvantage once you become accustomed to its use. High power units are best. Strobe lights tend to be more expensive but are ideal. They are ready-made for use underwater and do not require a housing.

To get the best results from flash you should take a test strip of exposures to enable you to make a chart of exposures suitable for medium to long distance use. Choose a subject, preferably in a swimming-pool during the evening when available light is less likely to overpower your flash. Measure 100cm to appear to give 75cm. Note each number used so that you can assess what F stop was used for the best exposure. This will give you a basis on which to work in the future, eg if F11 is best for 75cm then use F16 for 50cm (apparent).

Films

Most types of film can be used. For average light, high-speed Ektachrome or other high-speed film is most suitable. With a flash 25ASA and 50ASA films can be used. These have a finer grain and give sharper pictures.

Cine filming

Choose a light, neat, easy-to-operate camera. There are a number available which come complete with housing and stabilising fins. Automatic focusing and exposure remove two of the points you normally have to deal with before filming. The maximum pressure recommended for some housings is 40m. There are underwater cine cameras which can be used without any housing. Finding something suitable within your own price range should not be too difficult with the choice available today.

Use of camera
As with all underwater photography, always choose good visibility and try not to stir up silt on the bottom. Do not use the camera to take 'snapshots'. Have a theme in your mind and choose your subjects carefully to fit in with that theme. Filming in approximately ten-second bursts should be long enough for one sequence. Get as close to your subject as is possible. If filming other divers advise them beforehand, to make communication easier. Film from in front of them as their fins will kick up silt which will interfere with filming.

Films
A standard film can be used down to a depth of about five metres, eg 25ASA or equivalent. From 5–40m, high-speed Ektachrome or Fuji RT200 or equivalent can be used.

Before using a camera in the sea
Try out any camera you purchase in a swimming-pool before taking it into the sea. You will find plenty of divers only too happy to be recorded for posterity executing a forward roll.

Every time you take the camera in the sea check the housing for leaks as you descend. It may be necessary to tighten the screws on the housing as the 0-rings compress under pressure. If the housing is new take it down empty on a fairly deep dive (say thirty metres) for its first outing. Always load the camera with film in a clean dry place, eg in the car. Make sure the 0-ring seals are clean and undamaged and that they form a perfect seal every time.

Allow yourself plenty of time before diving to check your cameras, flash, housings, etc. Plan your dive based on what type of photography you intend to do.

As with all diving gear take care to wash off your camera equipment in fresh water after use.

To get results for your efforts you have to be a patient diver. You cannot economise on film or you will find you may have missed some really good shots by taking only one instead of two or three (if using a still camera). Filming fish is both fascinating and restful. If you lie quietly on the seabed they quickly get used to your presence and continue with their lives as if you were not there. Breaking up a sea-urchin on which they can feed allows you to get some good results. Anchor yourself amongst the kelp roots where the life is usually abundant. Some of the plant-life is truly beautiful and colourful around Britain, equal to anything seen in foreign waters. A flash on a still camera will bring out those colours. The magic is already there, you only need a little imagination and patience to capture it on film.

Archaeology

A number of important underwater sites have been found by chance. If you should come across an area which appears to be of interest do not remove anything from the site. Make a sketch map of it and drawings of any items noticed. Better still take some photographs. Take transit bearings or mark the site, preferably do both.

Contact an association or individual in the world of archaeology dealing with underwater discoveries so that a properly organised superficial survey can be made prior to possible excavation if the site proves worthwhile. The excavation can take years of painstaking work covering the site metre by metre investigating any piece of timber, bone, or artifact. All items have to be brought to the surface in case they are vital to the building-up of the picture. Each piece has to be expertly treated to prevent deterioration due to the action of salts once it is exposed to the air.

Not every ship is a treasure ship. Excavation can be a tedious way of spending your time. Sifting every particle of sand in case you miss some vital artifact, hardly moving from one spot during your dive time. The end result is still exciting and rewarding when all the evidence is pieced together and it is possible to tell which ship she was and when she went down, what kind of people travelled with her to the bottom of the ocean.

If you are interested there are lectures to be attended on archaeology and more and more books on the subject appear every year. Better still, there are various sites being worked on and it may be possible to join a team on a voluntary basis so that you can learn by experience.

14
Further Types of Diving

To enable you to become an experienced and knowledgeable diver you obviously have to try new things. New depths, diving in tides, working underwater, low visibility. However, it cannot be stressed too strongly that experience in these comes gradually. It also depends, to an extent, on what type of person you are. You may find low visibility diving is not to your taste or perhaps that you prefer to dive in less than thirty metres. In which case, dive within your own limitations. Do not allow yourself to go into situations with which you know you will be unable to cope. You could endanger someone else.

Deep diving

Depth in diving, with an ignorant few, is a status symbol. They talk incessantly about dives which increase in depth with each telling of the tale. One thing you will find out very quickly is that depth in itself means nothing. In fact, in less than twenty metres or so, you will find there is abundant life. In British waters, the deeper you go the more barren it tends to become. The colours in the light become absorbed so that at around twenty-five metres everything will be reduced to a blue–grey tinge.

Deep dives have to be planned thoroughly in advance. Decompression stops have to be taken into consideration. The size of cylinder(s), which you will require to ensure you do not run out of air while decompressing, has to be considered. The fitness of the diver is very important. If you are very overweight, run down, or have a hangover then you are better off leaving the deep one until some other time. Going into thirty metres or more you must consider the extra stamina you will need. Breathing may appear to become slightly more difficult. Providing you have a good demand valve you should not experience this to a marked degree. The compression of a wetsuit will mean some loss of heat insulation and buoyancy, at the same time there will be a drop in the water temperature.

Feelings of panic on land can, to a certain extent, be mastered. Likewise underwater you can cope with nervous tension. However, you must bear in mind that you cannot suddenly remove yourself from the spot, especially if decompression stops are involved. If something does unsettle you underwater then you may be better advised giving the signal to ascend immediately. Do not endanger yourself and/or your buddy by trying to stay down, rather ruin his dive by cutting it short. The worst that can happen then is that he will avoid diving on a deep one with you again.

If you do have to surface, do not let it put you off deep diving entirely. Try and work out what it was that caused the problem. It may be that you would be happier diving on deep reefs where the visibility is better. Perhaps you were much too heavy and consequently working hard just to get around. Your buddy, although very experienced, may have been unknown to you and this may have been the trouble. When trying new things it is a good idea, where possible, to dive with someone already known to you and in whom you have confidence. This has the effect of increasing your confidence in your own abilities and helping you to be more aware.

Planning a deep dive
The party of divers should be fairly small, preferably not more than six. Divers should be in pairs, not more. Keeping contact with one buddy is enough. The boat to be used should if possible be a 'hard' boat, with a dinghy available for

emergencies. The nearest recompression facilities should be noted. It is unwise to go deeper than 45–50m on compressed air.

At the site, the boat should anchor over the wreck or reef, putting down a shot line to the seabed as well. If there is likely to be any current, a buoyant line should be streamed astern. If a diver has trouble getting back to the boat it will give him something to hold on to while he is either pulled to the boat or fetched by dinghy. There should be no non-divers in the boat as they get in the way and do not serve any useful purpose. The boat handler should be experienced with diving parties or be a diver himself. A fully-kitted stand-by diver should be on the boat.

Divers should have built up to the deep dive. It is not sensible to go from regular dives in, say, 15m of water, to a dive of 30m. Before diving the pair should synchronise watches and plan duration and depth of dive plus depth and duration of decompression stops. Plans should not be changed once they are underwater. The correct amount of weight should be worn. If very overweight a fair amount of air will have to be used in the ABLJ to compensate. If too light difficulties may be experienced when carrying out decompression stops in that the diver will be too buoyant and will probably end up clinging to the line upside down. Gear should be checked and in good working order, as before any dive.

In the water, watches should be set immediately before descending the anchor line. Go down as quickly as possible allowing for equalisation of pressure on ears, mask, etc. At the bottom of the line both divers should check depth and exchange OK signals. In the decreased visibility it is important not to lose each other. Also you will want to find your way back to the anchor or shot line for decompression purposes. In some cases it may be a good idea to use a guideline run from the bottom of one of these lines so that you can get back easily within the specified time. Checks on depth and time should be kept to ensure pre-planning is adhered to and the signal to ascend exchanged at the appropriate time. Ascend at the normal rate with your buddy and carry out agreed stops. Surface and signal OK to the boatman. Times and depths should be recorded.

Wreck diving

First, it should be said that wreck dives should be thoroughly pre-planned. If it is a deep wreck dive then special attention must be paid to decompression stops and bottom time.

Some wrecks are well known and dived regularly. Luckily, for the novice diver, not all wrecks lie in very deep water. There are some lying in twenty metres or less which are very worthwhile visiting. In some cases the visibility is far better than that on the deeper wrecks. They are ideal on which to start building your experience. Shallow wrecks are more affected by storms and are usually widely scattered over the seabed. This particularly applies to old wooden ships which have disintegrated and have been covered gradually by sand or mud.

Deep water and wrecks often go hand in hand with low visibility, depending on the site. Mentally you have to prepare yourself for the visibility in which you start descending to reduce drastically, in some areas possibly to less than two or three metres. It becomes an eerie dark green gloom out of which dark shapes loom unexpectedly and sudden chasms open up beneath you. Swimming up the vast hull of a ship can be an unnerving experience when you do not really know where it starts or ends, but it does add to the excitement.

Generally speaking wrecks are, at whatever depth, unrecognisable as ships. The exceptions are some modern ships where it is possible to swim along a row of holes, where portholes once were, or down the massive hull.

Wreck diving is popular with a number of clubs. Apart from the obvious interest in investigating the remains of the ship, these remains do encourage marine life to flourish at depths where a reef might be barren. Some divers visit wrecks for the purpose of souvenir hunting. Apart from the desire to find valuable items they are prepared to spend time removing brass portholes and other items of interest. Working over thirty metres below the surface with a hammer and chisel invariably means they run very low on air. Other divers prefer to become involved in helping out with the recovery and preservation of artifacts from protected wreck sites.

Planning a wreck dive
Apart from the obvious preparations with regard to times you should make sure you are wearing a knife, as you should on any dive, and, preferably, carrying a torch. A torch is particularly useful for illuminating holds, under plates, etc, and attracting the attention of other divers. You will want to keep off the wreck as much as possible to avoid stirring up silt so a short handspear or similar will come in handy to support your weight.

A number of the wreck sites lie in areas very much affected by strong tides therefore the time of slack water becomes more critical than ever. The buoyant stern line is also an essential.

Following the normal procedures to the seabed you and your buddy then orientate yourselves. You may use parts of the wreck by which to find your way back to the anchor line or shot line. In very poor visibility it may be wise to attach a guideline but they can be a nuisance on a wreck. If inspecting the inside of the wreck use a line to your buddy outside to keep in touch. You may stir up silt inside and be unable to find your way out again. On the wreck take care not to damage your suit or your person. You will find gloves useful for protection from cuts on plates.

If a deep wreck, keep a close eye on depth, times, etc, to ensure surfacing with sufficient air for decompression stops. It is very easy to become engrossed on a wreck and the short time allowed slips by too quickly.

Note: If intending to remove objects from a wreck it is as well to check the legal position. In theory, all wrecks belong to a person or body of persons. It is, strictly speaking, not legal to 'salvage' without permission. Some wrecks are protected and on no account should items be removed from a wreck of this type.

Low visibility dive

Low visibility, that is one metre or less, should never be dived in by a novice. It should only be undertaken for a specific purpose, eg surveying a site, carrying out underwater maintenance, etc, and by very experienced divers.

Stringent safety precautions have to be taken. These include pre-arranged rope signals via a direct line to the diver from the fully kitted-up stand-by diver on the boat. A spare breathing set must be available. This type of diving is usually carried out by a lone diver rather than pairs. It is difficult enough to feel your way around without having the responsibility of a buddy. Also two divers are likely to get in the way of each other and may even dislodge equipment. The safest way to descend in this visibility is feet first. Being unable to see the bottom or the possible hazards you could easily land on your head. If your apparatus becomes snagged on something it is best to back away from the obstruction as the way you went in must have been free but the way ahead may be worse.

In the dense murk where unseen obstacles lie, the imagination can work very much overtime. Lying in grey-brown muddy water, the sound of air bubbling away through the exhaust valve, you are very much alone. You have to put your faith in the man at the other end of the rope. To dive in such circumstances has to have a worthwhile objective, it certainly is not 'fun'. Not all experienced amateur divers care to dive in such conditions.

Night diving

Diving at night is a unique and fascinating experience. It gives you the opportunity of seeing marine life you may not see during the daylight hours. Also you will be able to observe different patterns of behaviour in specimens already known to you. The fact that you use a torch will introduce the full spectrum of colours which is missing during the day. The true

143

colours, some brilliant, some delicate, spring to life under illumination. It gives you the chance to see them as they really are, a chance you do not otherwise get except in colour slides where a flash has been used.

Once you have become used to the renewed strangeness of the underwater world it adds to the experience to switch off the torches. In this way you can watch the phosphorescence shower from your moving limbs like sparks in the dark water. To get the full benefit of the dive move slowly and concentrate on studying the detail of the life around you.

Planning a night dive

The party should be kept small, diving only in pairs. Each diver must carry a torch of his own, strapped to his wrist. Buddy lines should be used to prevent the divers from being separated from each other. Both should wear compasses and take a bearing from the shore so that they do not swim for ever out to sea. Strict time-keeping should be observed so that the boat cover and/or shore cover will know immediately if you are overdue.

A night dive is best carried out on a site close to shore, within easy snorkelling distance. Better still, it should be a site already well known to the divers. Entry and exit of the water should be easy, preferably a gently sloping sand or shingle beach. The spot should be sheltered, the night calm, and there should be no strong tide running. The dive should be in less than twelve metres. A full moon certainly helps. It cuts down on torch waving on the beach, lost gear, etc. It also helps with coming ashore at exactly the right spot. Likewise it assists the emergency boat to keep an eye on surfacing divers.

The boat cover will have to avoid using its engine as the risk of injuring a surfacing diver with the rotating propeller is much increased in the dark. In an emergency a weighted flare sent down by the boat can be used to recall divers. Only in an emergency should the torch be used to signal the boat. Never wave the torch about on the surface as lights at sea could mislead the coastguard into thinking there is someone in trouble. If you wish to signal underwater shine your torch on your signal, never at your buddy. He will not be able to see anything at all for several minutes.

Before a night dive is carried out the local coastguard should be informed so that he is aware of the reasons for all the activity in the area. Even if it is a balmy summer night, make sure you have a flask of hot drink and some warm windproof clothing for after the dive.

Inland water diving

Numerous divers spend much of their time diving inland waters – lakes, quarries, etc. Some areas of inland water can be very interesting and well worth visiting. There are obvious differences between fresh and sea water diving but the safety aspects remain the same.

Fresh water is usually colder than sea water, depending on the effect of the season and the weather, the depth of water also being relevant. You will find yourself less buoyant in freshwater and will therefore require less lead on the weightbelt. Any necessary permission should be obtained before diving in the water site chosen.

Do not dive near locks, sluice gates, etc, as the suction can be strong enough to hold a diver underwater. Avoid fast-flowing rivers due to the risk of injury to self or equipment being dislodged by obstructions. If diving in a quarry avoid areas of possible rockfalls above water. All inland waters, with the possible exception of reservoirs, are unfortunately used as dumping grounds by the surrounding population. They are hazardous from the point of view of equipment snagging on old bedsteads, bicycles, etc. Rivers and canals should be dived with caution, not only from the point of view of rubbish but from a nasty clinging weed and possibly pollution. Visibility can be badly affected by the stirring up at a touch of the soft mud on the bottom.

Spearguns should not be used in inland waters. Also diving

under ice should not be undertaken by inexperienced amateurs.

Cave diving

This book is intended for those interested in finding out how to start learning to be a safe diver. Cave diving is a highly specialised subject that is best left out as it requires not only an experienced diver but a knowledgeable one. The occupation is fraught with innumerable extra hazards and has to be carried out under organised conditions. If you should be interested in taking part you would be well advised to join a cave diving club which will be able to assess whether or not you are the right material.

Diving in caves under the sea should also be undertaken only after careful planning and with the provision of ropes, guidelines, torches, etc as the following indicates.

Some very experienced divers did enter an undersea cave in excellent visibility. However, they did so on the spur of the moment, lured by curiosity. They had no guidelines rigged up and were not carrying torches. The sand was so fine that when it was stirred up one of them was unable to find the way out again, the visibility was so bad. Only by breathing from his life-jacket was he able to last out until he was found. He was given air and taken to the surface where he was lucky enough to recover. His rescuer might have been one minute longer in finding him.

Diving for a living

Having found you enjoy the exhilaration and sense of freedom you get from sport diving you may feel moved to consider diving for a living. If you regularly risk your life in the watery oil-fields of the world then you can earn a lot of money. Despite the tightening-up of safety regulations it is still very much a high-risk job.

At one time you could get a job as a deep diver practically just by signing on the dotted line. Today it is very different. Companies require proof of reliable qualifications and training undergone before considering a diver. There are courses available which, providing you are competent in training, issue certificates which are acceptable. Three of the schools which provide such courses in Britain are the Underwater Training Centre at Fort William, Fort Bovisand near Plymouth and Prodive Ltd, Charlestown, Cornwall.

Taking a course can cost you a great deal of money. Alternatively, you may be lucky enough to be accepted for sponsorship by the government under the TOPS scheme which enables people to train or retrain in various employments. Before being accepted for a TOPS course you will have to be over nineteen years of age and have a BSAC (British Sub-Aqua Club) 2nd class diver qualification. Also required is some skill or experience in a practical field such as engineering, welding, shipbuilding or similar. You will also have to pass a stiff medical. If over thirty years of age you must have previous commercial diving experience – cutting, welding, explosives, etc. If not being sponsored some schools will accept you at eighteen years of age.

The three month course for basic trainees aims to bring them to a standard of competency in a complete range of work underwater in varying conditions, down to fifty metres using different types of equipment.

There is also a six week course available for those already experienced as work divers (minimum twelve months). This course covers the use of mixed gases, submersible compression chambers, saturation diving, etc.

Any diver with rose-tinted notions about the romance attached to being a pro-diver, must find himself quickly disillusioned with his first leap off the end of the quay at Fort Bovisand into a fairly lumpy sea. Divers can and often do resign from the course before the end. Often it is found necessary to advise a trainee he is unsuitable and must leave. In this case he is always warned in advance and helped before this final step is taken.

There are other opportunities to work underwater, eg marine biology, photography and archaeology. However, they are rare even though you might have the right qualifications and are an experienced diver. Some divers make a living freelance working as diving instructors part of the year or moving to other countries where they can support themselves in this way all the year round. It is possible to earn a living by underwater fishing. Some work underwater salvaging brass, copper, etc, from more modern wrecks. Some work on wreck recovery, bringing coins and artifacts for preservation and eventual auctioning or placing in museums. A handful of divers have possibly earned quite large amounts of money in this field but the type of wrecks which carry vast sums in coins are few and far between. The work and time involved in tracing the wreck costs a great deal of money and the number of people able to finance such operations over a long period is small.

A further gloomy note is that most work underwater is exacting and the working life of a diver is comparatively short. You may have to be prepared to look for other ways of earning a living when in your forties.

Appendix

Learning to dive

There are three ways of learning to dive, through:
1 The British Sub-Aqua Club or other Diving Club or Association.
2 A commercially-run diving school.
3 A friend.
You could just read a few chapters of a book and then walk into the water. This is most definitely *not recommended*.

To take point three first – *do not*. The friend might be a good diver but he will not be experienced in showing someone else. He could miss out a vital piece of theory or practice. He may not be aware of discomfort or growing panic in you in a particular situation until it is too late. Not fatal perhaps but enough to put you off diving for ever. False courage may prevent you from telling a friend of something which worries you underwater and which could easily be dealt with if known about. Properly trained a diver will be equipped to deal with most situations calmly.

Commercially-run schools
These are growing in numbers for sport diving and, within their limitations, can be good. Some people cannot, at first, face the thought of the long rigorous training demanded by most clubs. A school provides a short-cut introduction to diving in the sea. The general format seems to be:

1 Evening sessions in a pool and lectures. After a specified period these are usually followed by sea dives at weekends.
2 One week or more 'holiday' intensive training which includes lectures, pool training and sea dives. The depths of the dives will depend on the ability of the individual.

The disadvantage with these methods is that, although you probably get the basic information and training, the lack of time available does not give you the varied experience under expert guidance which enables you to cope with possible problems underwater and on the surface. A school may encourage you to continue with pool sessions at the end of training. This costs money but is well worth it to keep in practice. A novice can quickly become ill-at-ease in his equipment, after quite a short time. Also it is worth arranging with the school to pay extra for more sea dives accompanied by an experienced diver.

The advantage of learning in this manner is that it does give you an insight into the underwater world. It can act as a spur to go on with your training and gain experience and knowledge, possibly by joining a club, which is certainly the best way of ensuring you have someone with whom to dive each weekend.

Diving clubs
Learning with a club is generally considered to be much the safest way to learn to dive, albeit necessarily long-winded. The benefits far outweigh the deficits.

In Britain the largest club is the British Sub-Aqua Club (BSAC) and they also have branches in other parts of the world. Their standard of training is exceptionally high. It demands a reliable level of stamina and swimming ability before it will take you as a snorkel diver. To some extent how fast you progress will be up to you although they do have a planned programme of lectures and pool training which is followed. Normally the course starts in about October and proceeds through the winter – a good way of getting and keeping fit for the diving season as a number of people often spend the dark evenings slumped unhealthily in front of a TV. By the time the warmer weather comes you should be through your basic training and working towards your 3rd Class qualification as an aqualung diver.

The number of clubs which are non-BSAC is growing year by year and these also generally require a good standard of thorough training before a novice is considered safe. If you work with concentration and enthusiasm you will find the instructors and other club members only too happy to help you with advice, even extra coaching in the pool. You will also find more of them prepared to help you with your sea snorkelling and aqualung dives if you show commonsense, reliability, and are obviously conscious of the safety aspects.

Apart from the training there are other benefits from belonging to a club. There is the use of a boat or a party with whom to hire a 'hard' boat, training in boat-handling and numerous courses available for study of marine biology, archaeology, photography, advanced diving techniques, etc. When diving abroad most places require a certificate before hiring or filling cylinders. Clubs dive mid-week evenings if possible and most weekends. Many arrange trips to various parts of the coast for diving holidays. There is usually someone prepared to dive with you who shares your particular interest. There is always someone from whom to learn, be it about diving, equipment or boats.

When belonging to a club of any sort you have to pull your weight. There are boats and engines to be maintained, hire equipment to be collected and returned, funds to be raised and general organisation with which to be involved. Once you have gained enough experience you can put something back into the club by helping to train other novices.

Diver's code

The BSAC and other clubs have agreed codes for their divers to follow. You may not belong to any club and therefore do not feel particularly responsible. Remember though that there are hundreds of divers using various inland and coastal sites. They do not all belong to clubs but if all sport divers act in a responsible manner then the bad name they have had in the past can gradually be improved. The following is a list of do's and don'ts which may act as a guide.

Please don't

1 Don't dive within harbour limits, in private water, or use private accesses to dive sites without first asking permission.
2 Don't cause obstruction or annoyance to non-divers by parking vehicles badly, or by littering large areas of beach, slipway or car park with diving gear. Don't obstruct slipways with boat trailers.
3 Don't use a portable compressor where the noise is likely to give offence.
4 Don't cause damage to property or leave litter.
5 Don't dive in fairways or busy 'shipping' areas. Large boats cannot alter course or speed quickly, neither should they be expected to go out of the recognised channel, possibly at risk to their own safety. You may also put yourself in danger, particularly when surfacing.
6 Don't interfere with, or dive in close proximity to, fishermen's lines, nets, or pots.
7 Don't take berried crabs or lobsters, or fish or shellfish below minimum size*. Don't flaunt your catch on the beach or quay and don't take more than you need to eat.
8 Don't use a speargun with an aqualung. Don't use a speargun (if snorkelling) close to other divers or in fresh water.
9 It is illegal to remove articles from wrecks without first consulting the owners. Do not vandalise protected wrecks.

Please do

1 Promote goodwill between divers and other water users, particularly fishermen. Be prepared to help them by freeing

propellers, checking moorings, etc.
2 Use a reliable boat and boat handler.
3 Fly the diver's flag as a warning while the dive is in progress.
4 Observe the rules of safety in relation to diving and boats. Avoid endangering your own life and/or that of someone who may have to come to your assistance.
5 Be conservation-minded.

Note: Minimum sizes vary but do not take plaice less than 25cm; sole less than 24cm; turbot 30cm. Crabs must be at least 115cm across the broadest part of the shell, lobsters at least 80mm carapace measured from rear of eye socket to rear end of body shell. Berried lobsters and berried or soft crabs are in spawn so should not be taken. Minimum size for scallops is approx. 10cm. There are minimum sizes laid down for free-swimming fish as well as flat fish.

Safety

Safety is a word which seems to appear, emphasised, on at least every other page of this book. Diving can be a hazardous sport although very few divers suffer serious injury of any kind unless they are ignorant or take stupid risks. All the following points are mentioned elsewhere in the book but a few reminders do no harm.

Training
Before using an aqualung seek proper training. Listen to, and remember, what you are told. Never think you know it all. Practise in the pool regularly even after you feel competent with your equipment. In the sea continue to do as you are requested. Your instructor knows far more about boats, tides, winds, etc, in relation to diving, than you do at this stage.

After training
You still do not know it all. Knowledge comes with experience, do not try to rush things.

Sea diving

1 Always check your equipment before use. Make sure you turn on your air and check your demand valve yourself.
2 Check state of tide and weather conditions.
3 If shore diving check entry and exit points. Make sure you are diving on a site which is within the range of your stamina. Conserve some air in case of problems on the return swim.
4 If using a boat check equipment and, if in doubt with regard to weather conditions, do not go. It is difficult and dangerous retrieving scattered divers from a rough sea. It may be impossible.
5 Always take a marker buoy so that your boat cover can keep track of you.
6 Never dive outside your limitations, eg if deep wrecks worry you, do not bother with them. Discomfort interferes with concentration. Do not encourage someone else to take risks, you may not be as competent as you think to help them when they get into trouble.
7 Dives should always be pre-planned. Never enter an underwater cave without the necessary planning. Do not suddenly decide to carry out a decompression dive when you originally intended to stay within, say, twenty metres.
8 When diving on a wreck never enter it without being sure of your exit. A line to a buddy outside is a sensible safety measure.
9 Do not try to concentrate on more than one aspect of diving at a time. Visiting a deep wreck festooned not only with cameras but underwater torch and tools increases the hazards enormously.
10 Practise life-saving techniques and EAR until you are competent.

Bibliography

There are now dozens of books written on various aspects of life under the sea. A brief selection is suggested below which may be of interest or assistance.

Marine archaeology

Bass, George F. *Archaeology Underwater* Thames & Hudson 1966
Du Platt Taylor, Joan. *Marine Archaeology* Hutchinson 1965
McKee, Alexander. *History Under the Sea* Hutchinson 1968
Magnusson, Magnus. *Introducing Archaeology* Bodley Head 1972
Stenuit, Robert. *Treasures of the Armada* David & Charles 1972
Wilkes, B. St John. *Nautical Archaeology* David & Charles 1971

Marine biology

Barratt, John and Yonge, Charles M. *Pocket Guide to the Sea Shore* Collins 1979
Campbell, A. C. *Hamlyn Guide to the Seashore* and *Shallow Seas of Britain and Europe* Hamlyn Publishing Company 1976
Friedrich, H. *Marine Biology*
de Haas, W. and Knorr, F. *Young Specialist Looks at Marine Life* Burke 1966
MacGinitie, G. and MacGinitie, N. *The Natural History of Marine Animals* McGraw 1968
Nicol, J. A. C. *The Biology of Marine Animals*
Tait, R. V. *Elements of Marine Ecology* Butterworth 1972
Woods, J. P. and Lythgoe, J. N. *Underwater Science*

BIBLIOGRAPHY

Seamanship, etc

Watkins, C. G., *Coastwise Navigation* Kandy Publications
Reed's Nautical Almanac and Tide Tables, T. Reed 1976
The Mariner's Handbook The Hydrographic Department

You will find that articles in diver-related magazines are often very informative and usually give titles of books which may be of interest to you.

Index

INDEX

INDEX

INDEX